Human-centred design for IT service management

Katrina Macdermid

Published by TSO (The Stationery Office), part of the
Williams Lea group of companies.

Mail, Telephone & Email:
TSO
PO Box 29, Norwich, NR3 1GN
Telephone orders/General enquiries: 0333 202 5070
Email: customer.services@tso.co.uk Textphone 0333 202 5077

www.tsoshop.co.uk

Second edition 2023
ISBN print 9780117094376
ISBN PDF 9780117094383
ISBN ePub 9780117094390

SD000049

Contents

About the author

This book is about you. Yes, that's right, it's about you. But before I explain why this is so important, I'll tell you a little about me.

I'm one of the lucky ones to have found success by being forced to reimagine my business during one of the most challenging times in recent history – the Covid-19 pandemic. It's something I'm grateful for every day. And yet during this unsettling period I couldn't stop a rather niggling and persistent thought that kept rearing its head: why don't you write a book?

You see, I fundamentally believe that we have a problem in IT service management. Or should I say 'problems'? For example, when was the last time you heard someone say, 'Our IT department is fantastic'? Yet despite the many frameworks IT professionals subscribe to, as they're finding their role in another IT restructure, working on a new IT service management tool, being involved in initiatives to improve their processes, and reading consultancy recommendations on how to transform, my belief is this: *IT service management is broken.*

And that thought leads me to ask:

- How do we change decades-old IT service management processes?
- How do we change tired and outdated IT support models?
- And how do we change the mindset and ways of working of the people responsible for IT service management?

The answer is: by *Humanising IT™*.

We have created a unique, innovative and much-needed overhaul to IT service management called 'Humanising IT™'. This aims to educate and inform all IT professionals on the 'how' and the 'why' of what IT service management should be. It will show you how and why you must put people at the heart of your IT service management to design and support IT services that your users will love, and that your IT people will love designing and supporting.

Where it started

In 2019, I had my dream job. I was co-chair and adviser of a board representing some 300 of the world's airlines. For two years, I led the transformation of IT support models and service level agreements between the airlines and their service providers. The job enabled me to travel, meet leading experts in their fields, work in new and exciting industries, and immerse myself in varied workplace cultures. No matter where I was in the world, no matter which industry I worked in, no matter what kind of workplace culture they ascribed to, everybody reported the same problems: business people were unhappy with IT, and IT people felt disengaged from the business.

Having worked on both sides of the divide (in business and IT), I knew that when it came to delivering IT services, people in IT had the right intentions. They were hard-working and passionate about doing a good job. But they felt disempowered. Meanwhile, people on the business side were frustrated by their IT departments. They cited long wait times, complicated solutions and less-than-optimum user experience. Business people couldn't understand why the service from their IT department was so uniformly poor.

And then Covid-19 hit.

Like the rest of the world, my travelling days were over, at least for a while. But it was especially painful for me because of my long-standing love of the aviation industry and the people who worked in it. I saw many of my colleagues lose their jobs and face increasing economic uncertainty, along with fears about their health and families. As the saying among us goes, the jet fuel gets into your blood.

Of course, aviation wasn't the only industry that was hard hit. The repercussions of Covid-19 were being felt across the board and around the globe. I knew I had to pivot, just like so many people were doing. The crisis gave me time to think about how I could best use my knowledge and skills to continue doing what I loved.

An unexpected perspective

For those of you who know me, you will know that I love a challenge and strive to be the best I can possibly be. Back in 2016, Qantas Airways sponsored my certification to become an ITIL® Master at a time when there were only two others in Australia. To qualify, I studied more than 5000 pages of IT service management publications. But I also had the good fortune to be studying human-centred design at the same time – almost by accident.

As I started to synthesise the ideas from both human-centred design and IT service management, I began to question why we weren't taking a more human approach to designing and supporting IT services. One thing that struck me about those 5000 pages while studying was that there wasn't a single picture of a human being. Sure, lots of diagrams of processes illustrating inputs, outputs, touchpoints, roles etc.; however, not one single image of a human.

So, who were these IT services being managed for? And who was managing them?

If it hadn't been for the happy coincidence of my dual studies, I may never have noticed how both human-centred design and IT service management strive to achieve the same outcomes (but approach them in completely different and contradictory ways), and this book may never have been written. I almost certainly would have continued to shout from my soapbox that the traditional view of IT service management best practice was best. I would not have questioned my decades-held belief that this was the right way to manage IT services. 'Follow the process' (and don't deviate) was my mantra.

Integrating human-centred design into IT service management

Human-centred design is about empathising with the human experience. But it falls short when understanding IT service management and the inherent complexity required to deliver the human experience. Whereas IT service management focuses on delivering value (and to some extent experience), it doesn't make use of some of the most powerful tools and techniques available for understanding and shaping the human experience – tools that are used in human-centred design, such as empathy, research and personas.

Human-centred design isn't equipped to address IT concepts such as availability, response times or software patching requirements. Conversely, IT service management doesn't have a way to determine how response times are impacting user stress levels (or the resulting stress for IT professionals). And neither of them uses empathy to understand IT professionals (in other words, you and me). It's always about the customer or the user.

Let's go back to 2016 – the period when I was studying human-centred design at the same time as my ITIL Master. Studying human-centred design involved attending classes at a college in Sydney, Australia. One Saturday morning, as I was listening to my tutor explain the concepts of human-centred design, I had the rather precarious thought 'Why don't we use these concepts in IT service management?' And that's where it all started – my idea of Humanising IT™.

Tell me a story

One of my favourite tools in the human-centred design toolbox is something we've all grown up doing: telling a story. We use stories to understand and explain the world around us. We naturally make up stories from our experiences, and we understand our experiences best when we can create a meaningful story that pulls together the relevant details into a coherent and memorable narrative.

One of the stories I have written is about a popular IT service management framework. The storyline follows a realistic (but fictional) team of IT professionals as they implement the framework into their business. Students follow the challenges and successes my characters face, which provides a human side to their learning (so it is not just about processes, inputs and outputs). The characters are presented as people rather than faceless, process-following cyphers, and readers are encouraged to empathise with them as they adopt and adapt the framework (which results in both success and some missed opportunities).

Making a human connection

Contributing to books and white papers on IT service management, and sharing the stage with some of the most experienced professionals, has given me a profound perspective and a deep appreciation for all those who work in this area. I've been able to develop relationships with the world's leading experts in the field, who are still my good friends to this day. I now consult and educate around the world, and I've met people from all walks of life: from those who work for international and publicly listed financial institutions, to those whose jobs are with health service providers and in the public sector.

I also have a regular blog and podcast, *Humanising IT*, where my guests are respected thought leaders from across the globe. My podcasts provide a valuable platform for guests to voice learnings, provide advice and share their experiences in IT service management. My goal is to break down the barriers, not just between businesses and IT departments, but within IT departments themselves, by making IT leaders available to a wider audience. I love asking these leaders questions that provoke and inspire.

More often than not, I'm able to persuade my guests to drop their guard and tell me what they really think about life, leadership and working in IT. They have all impressed and inspired me with their thoughtfulness and care. In many respects, they embody what it is to be a 'servant leader'. They will be the last to eat a meal, because they make sure that their teams are fed first. And yet, in every interview and post, every training course, every consultation and engagement I've done, I'm discovering that the problems we're facing today are the same as the ones we've always had: business people aren't happy with IT services, and IT people feel disengaged from the business. Something is still missing.

A problem of leadership

If I'm going to be honest, many of the leaders I interview are too far removed from the ground floor of IT service management. After all, it's been a long time since they've worked there (if they've worked there at all). Time, and technology, have moved on. The rate of change has accelerated, and expectations have evolved – not just the expectations of customers and users, but the expectations people have for their jobs and lifestyles. IT leaders often don't understand the challenges, fears and aspirations of their own people (that includes the service desk analysts, developers, process owners and product managers).

Perhaps that's not the job of our leaders. They're there to steer the ship in the right direction, not to work each one of the many oars. So, whose job is it to understand the people we serve, and us, the people doing the serving? Perhaps that job belongs to each one of us.

About this book

If you're reading this book, you probably want practical, actionable tools to help you in your IT service management career and learning pathways. You want to know how, specifically, to foster and manage relationships so you can get the best possible outcomes for your customers and colleagues. Good news! That's what this book is about.

Since I obtained my certification as an ITIL® Master, there's been a steady stream of books about service management, service metrics, operating models and new ways of working. However, there's rarely any discussion of the human experience. Not just the human experience of the end users, businesses and customers (more about that later) as they use the IT services, but the human experience of the IT people designing and supporting the services.

You can have the best metrics and the best-designed processes in the world, but if you're not using the tools and techniques of human-centred design, you could be missing a structured, imaginative and innovative approach to IT service management. Even if you're familiar with value stream mapping in IT service management, and even if you already know a thing or two about human-centred design, you'll find something new in this book.

This book is not an academic tome full of weighty theorising and ponderous but impractical advice. It is a book that tells a story – many stories, in fact. Storytelling is a crucial component of human-centred design and is the key to meaningful learning. For example, you may be surprised at how many lessons can be drawn from a story about a peanut butter sandwich. You may cackle at the beginnings of Fordism and be inspired by JFK's meeting with a janitor (at least, I hope you will be). You may also relate to stories about a kitchen and a chef. And throughout, I'll introduce you to the characters of Fly First Airlines, a fictitious story I've developed for my training and coaching. But be warned: there's some light-hearted humour and even a bit of flippancy sprinkled throughout. I'll also ask you to reflect on your own experiences as you progress through the book.

Don't be fooled by the fancy title of this book. I may be one of the few ITIL Masters in the world, but I'm not an academic and I don't aspire to be one. Instead, I've written this book in layperson's terms, for anyone who has a role in the management of IT services – from service desk analysts and software developers to CIOs and every human in between.

Who this book is for

This book is for you. You've come to the right place if you:

- Want to design and support IT services that bring about desired business outcomes and realise your organisation's vision (a vital consideration in Humanising IT)
- Aim to improve and nurture professional relationships with the people you serve (and the people who serve you)
- Seek to champion your IT department to the business (and the world!)
- Need to establish, understand, interpret and track key performance indicators (KPIs) for the human experience
- Plan to apply the concept of value stream mapping in IT service management, with a focus on the human experience
- Have a professional interest in industry shifts and sea changes resulting from IT services being increasingly embedded in distributed business models
- Are looking to set yourself apart in an increasingly competitive IT market
- Are interested in learning more about successful IT service management and the value of prioritising the human experience.

In this book, I'll show you how and why you can put people at the heart of your IT service management, so you can design and deliver services that your users will love, and that your IT people will love supporting.

I know you'll find something to entertain and educate you in these pages, and I invite you to share it with your colleagues and management.

How to use this book

The book is the companion resource to the accredited course, Humanising IT – human-centred design for IT service management.

In this book, I'll show you how human-centred design concepts can help you to design and support IT services. You'll learn some of the fundamental human-centred design concepts and discover how they overlap with and can complement IT service management concepts and frameworks. Throughout its pages, you'll find stories from international thought leaders who share their rich and diverse experiences to inspire and teach you how to take a human-centred approach to your work. I'll also provide you with some definitions of terms so you can use a shared language with your colleagues, customers and users. Finally, I'll show you a new way to design value streams that are focused on IT service management.

This book is not a replacement for specialist texts in human-centred design or IT service management. Instead, it brings a practical lens and storytelling approach to integrating and immediately applying these concepts in your workplace. It can also be a valuable resource for non-IT professionals seeking to develop their understanding of IT service management.

This is a foundational approach to human-centred design and IT service management. Further publications will provide the in-depth knowledge required to design and deliver IT services and value streams that integrate human-centred design.

Acknowledgements

I wanted my book not only to be educational but also to provide unique insights into the world of IT service management.

The wonderful humans below have helped me to create this book. Not only are they colleagues and mentors, but they are also my dear friends who have provided support and a shoulder to cry on, and shown confidence in me that this book could be written. My particular thanks go to my sister, Vicki, whose love and support have been invaluable.

Contributors

 Barry Anderson – Principal strategist, and adviser

 Chris Dolphin – Customer success executive

 Chris Barrett – Transformation specialist, board adviser, educationalist

 Vicki Macdermid – TEDx speaker, creator of EQiLead, board adviser

 Mark Basham – Chief executive, investor, board adviser

 Phillip Palmer – Service orchestration evangelist

 Deborah Biancotti – Editor and writer of narratives

 Ben Reid – Director of ICT service delivery, Sydney local health district

 Michael Buist – Adjunct professor, University of Tasmania

 Tobias Robinson – Service designer, human-centred designer, architect, multidisciplinary designer

Publisher's acknowledgements

TSO would like to thank David Barrow of DFBarrow Ltd and Tanya Rodahl of Rodahl Consulting for reviewing the manuscript and providing expert feedback. Their contributions have been very valuable and much appreciated by author and publisher.

1 IT service management culture and the challenges of today

 In this chapter, we will:

- Discuss technology today
- Examine IT culture (or the lack thereof)
- Explore how business people view IT service management
- Take a look at what we really do in IT (it's not just about machines and software)
- Start connecting IT culture with the human experience of those who use IT services
- Find a deeper purpose in IT service management.

Bridging the great divide

I am sure you will agree that technology has changed everything. From the moment we wake up until we go to sleep – and every moment in between – technology permeates our lives. The smartwatch with built-in biomonitoring, the self-driving vehicles, the home devices that optimise lighting, climate control and security, and the evolving smart cities: technology is everywhere. It has changed how, when and where we work and learn and how we interact with each other.

As our technological reliance grows, the management of technology services becomes increasingly complex – from banking to health, to law enforcement, to government. The complexity of the technology landscape, combined with our changing expectations of what technology can do for us, is compelling IT service management professionals to take a different approach.

IT service management was historically designed for stability, cost-effectiveness and standardisation. It was not designed to support – or even consider – the human experience. However, for IT departments to stay relevant to their users, they can no longer support just the technology. They must support people.

In IT service management, the word 'service' is usually a noun. It's about 'a' service. It isn't about serving. Netflix, for example, is a 'streaming service'. When referring to a 'service outage', we don't mean 'we've stopped serving you'. We mean the network is down. But what if we reimagined IT service management as 'in the service of'? What if we thought about the framework and delivery of IT service management as being designed to serve? Then we must ask a potentially frightening question: who or what are we serving? The answer is: we are serving the users.

Why is that important? When we understand our users, we can design services to match their needs and enable them to serve *their* customers' needs. And this needs to happen before we spend a thing on expensive prototyping, gratuitous consultancies, or convoluted service level agreements that few people can understand or bear to read.

This is a radical shift in thinking for IT service management. It turns the delivery and support of technology into a genuine customer-focused activity by putting the human experience at the centre of IT service management.

So, how do we do this? How do we change decades-old IT service management processes? How do we change tired and outdated IT support models? And how do we change the mindset and ways of working of the people responsible for IT service management?

The answer is *Humanising IT.*

Before we begin (we'll talk about the end)

In 'Who this book is for', we extended an invitation to share the contents and learning from this book with management and the broader business as an IT professional. Why is that important? We believe there is a fundamental disconnect between many businesses and what is understood as the role of IT service management.

The reasons are varied, and it is necessary to examine some of them to ensure we can take steps to make a change. So, we will explore some of the reasons, including the historical foundations of the frameworks adopted in IT service management, and the skills and attributes of those traditionally drawn to work in this space. And we will look at the challenges of definitions – same words, different meaning – and perceptions or misconceptions.

Organisational theorists would posit that the presence of disconnect and/or absence of harmony is an outcome of the culture. This is now a perfect opportunity to introduce Mark Basham (see box); his view is that IT culture is separated from the business (and this needs to change).

The importance of meaning

If you are reading this, I assume you understand what IT service management is. But let's spend some time discussing it, just to be sure we are all using the same meaning.

Many companies are service-based organisations, as opposed to being manufacturers (companies that create and ship goods). Service-based companies deliver services and include industries in the financial, aviation and healthcare sectors – to name but a few. IT service management is the sub-sector of these service-based industries that provides the IT resources.

Let's look at Fly First Airlines, a fictional story that I introduced in 'About this book'. The airline is a service-based industry transporting passengers and cargo. Examples of IT resources are hardware, software, people, specialised buildings, networks, etc. These IT resources need to be managed and that's where IT service management comes in.

It is important to note that there are many types of approaches – typically called frameworks – that are used to manage IT resources. IT service management covers the end-to-end delivery of IT services to customers, including all processes and activities to design and support IT services.[1] And, just to ensure a clear understanding (because it's in the title of the book), I've given a definition of human-centred design.

 Definition: Human-centred design

'Human-centered design is an approach to problem-solving [commonly used in design and management frameworks] that develops solutions to problems by involving the human perspective in all steps of the problem-solving process. Human involvement typically takes place in observing the problem within context, brainstorming, conceptualising, developing, and implementing the solution.'[2]

---

1   Atlassian. What is IT service management (ITSM)? https://www.atlassian.com/itsm.

2   Co-Creating Well-Being (Health Foundation for Western and Central New York). What is human-centered design? https://www.cocreatingwellbeing.com/research-hcd.

IT culture: A discussion by Mark Basham

Mark Basham, former CEO of Axelos; founder and director of HIT Global

Strategy and culture are among the primary levers available to top leaders in their quest to drive business performance and create sustainable success.[3] Strategy offers a formal logic for a company's goals and orients people around them.[4] Culture expresses goals through values, beliefs and ethics, and guides activity through shared assumptions, social norms and behaviours.[5]

Surveys consistently reinforce the importance of organisational culture to business performance and sustainable success. I fervently agree with whoever came up with the saying 'Culture will eat strategy for breakfast.'[6]

If teams are not aligned around a common set of values, beliefs and behaviours (culture), even the best strategy will be difficult to execute and risks outright failure.

Given the importance of culture to business performance and the delivery of strategy, it is surprising that so little is written about what makes a successful IT service management culture. IT service management frameworks have started to mention value and value creation but remain light on human experience, people and culture.

As I talk to IT executives in organisations across the globe, I am struck by the number of IT teams who still feel separated from the business. This separation inevitably results in IT culture being defined by the values, beliefs and shared norms of the people working in IT, who in all likelihood see themselves as passive contributors to culture.

This highlights two opportunities. Firstly, how do we help the IT service management teams to understand what a successful IT service management culture looks like within an organisation? And secondly, how do we ensure that the IT service management culture is aligned and integrated with the wider organisational culture?

Getting this right has the potential to unlock a massive upside to businesses and to transform the internal perception and position of the IT service management team, from cost centre and service provider to strategic business partner.

 Over to you

How would you describe the culture of your IT department?

Is that consistent with the overall organisation?

Do you see yourself as a passive or active contributor to your IT service management culture?

---

3   Adam Brandenburger. Strategy needs creativity.
     https://hbr.org/2018/01/whats-your-organizations-cultural-profile?ab=seriesnav-spotlight.

4   Boris Groysberg *et al.* What's your organization's cultural profile?
     https://hbr.org/2018/01/whats-your-organizations-cultural-profile?ab=seriesnav-spotlight.

5   The culture factor. https://hbr.org/2018/01/the-culture-factor.html.

6   Saying often attributed to Peter Drucker.

It's time to talk

Mark provides an executive's perspective of an IT department: do you know how the people in your business would describe your IT department?

Our research shows clear themes, in industries ranging from aviation to healthcare. Take a look at the word cloud in Figure 1 to see their answers. Can you relate to these responses? What stands out to you?

Figure 1 Word cloud – what does the business think of IT?

Over to you

Do you think you would receive the same responses if you asked your business what it thought of IT?

Complicated? Slow? Expensive?

These are words frequently used to describe how we think the business sees us as IT professionals. You may have even heard them used to describe us directly, in feedback surveys or messaged in a virtual meeting. So, if you think the business sees you negatively, you're not alone. Surveys of hundreds of IT service management professionals support the negative sentiments expressed above.

Veterans of the IT field know there's often a disconnect between business outcomes and the organisation's mission, and what the IT department is focusing on. A large percentage of our daily efforts involve working reactively, rather than proactively engaging with the business to identify opportunities to support – or even enhance – business outcomes and the organisation's mission.

A look at queues: IT issues versus innovation requests

The cost of managing incidents

IT is a huge part of the budget for many companies, and the money spent on IT is intended to create business value and support business growth, but *many IT organisations spend a large part of this budget on managing incidents.*

What do the customers of IT get in return for this investment? At best they get a reduction in the amount of business disruption that they suffer as a result of service failures. It's never going to be easy to say to your customers, 'We've done a fantastic job managing incidents, what contribution did this make to your business growth?' because customers expect you to resolve incidents; simply managing them doesn't add value to them or their business processes.

HDI[7]

But whoever asks IT professionals what they think of the business? Many IT people feel that there's little relationship between business expectations and acknowledgement of how IT positively supports business outcomes and the organisation's mission.

In our surveys, participants often report that they do not feel part of the business they serve. Instead, they feel that there's an 'us and them' mentality, with battle lines drawn, territories defended and various 'None shall pass!' signals littering the divide between IT and the business. Can we fix it?

---

7   HDI (Informa Tech). Why you should do less incident management.
     https://www.thinkhdi.com/en/library/supportworld/2016/do-less-incident-management.aspx.

Over to you

What's your experience of your IT department's alignment with your business outcomes?

What's your experience of your IT department's alignment with your organisation's mission?

The cost of confusion

Independent surveys show that the lack of clarity and alignment between IT service management and the business comes at a substantial cost.

The cost of failing to execute strategy

The world of business today is one of constant change. Complexity inside organisations is growing at an unprecedented rate. Leaders, managers and employees are under pressure to perform amidst uncertainty, inefficiency, and confusion.

Fewer than one-third of senior executives' direct reports clearly understand the connections between corporate priorities; this number plummets to 16% for frontline supervisors and team leaders.

For the average Global 2000 company, lack of alignment and confusion can cost $225 million or more each year in lost productivity.

XPLANE[8]

The statistics quoted by XPLANE reveal an enormous financial cost to the business. It's noteworthy that XPLANE includes 'confusion' as one of the sources of the costs. Confusion may be due to unclear vision, disconnected strategy and inconsistent processes, leading to painful experiences for customers and employees, and a toxic culture where there's disharmony between colleagues in the workplace who aren't united in a common goal. Without any disrespect to the traditional approach taken by consulting firms, rolling out another PowerPoint presentation and transformation project will never be the answer.

Figure 2 may be a parody, but it sadly represents many organisations' reality. For IT professionals, it's often amplified because they already feel disconnected from both the business and its customers, and they aren't given a clear sense of how they should support business outcomes and their organisation's mission.

---

8   XPLANE. Confusion vs. clarity poster. https://xplane.com/worksheets/confusion-vs-clarity-poster/. Calculations based on average employee size and compensation.

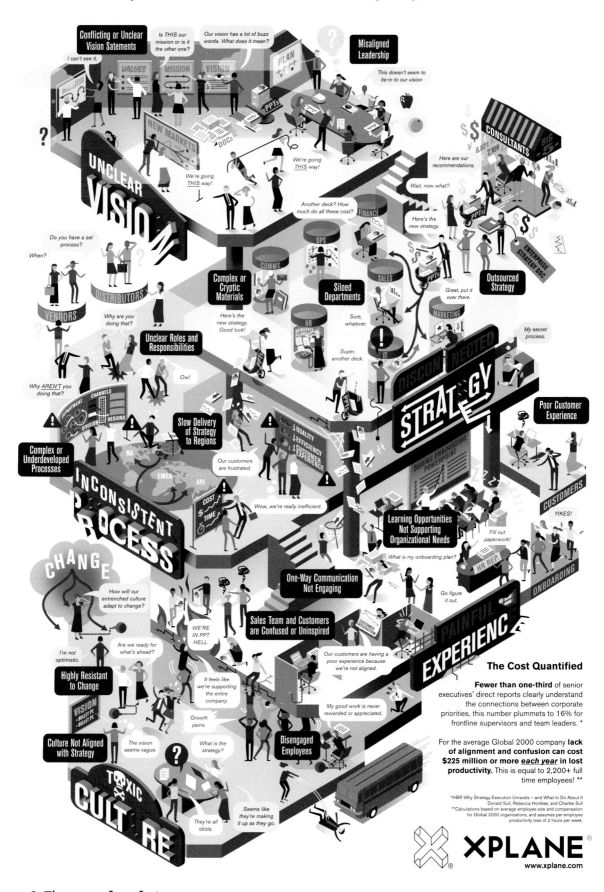

Figure 2 The cost of confusion
Courtesy of XPLANE

 Over to you

Although the illustration is directed at organisations as a whole, we love this graphic for the way it can be related to IT service management, with common themes and sentiments often heard (or whispered, texted or tweeted):

- Inconsistent processes
- Unclear vision
- Not another slide deck!
- Unclear roles and responsibilities
- Our mission has a lot of buzz words – what does it mean?
- Our customers are having a poor experience because we are not aligned
- Seems like they are making it up as they go.

Can you relate?

So why the disconnect?

To answer this question, it helps to understand the history of IT departments within organisations. Although it seems unimaginable, less than 40 years ago, a 'desktop' computer was a novelty and not the essential equipment we consider it to be today. In large organisations, mainframe installations dominated, serviced by highly specialised technicians. However, as computers became more popular and necessary business items, companies needed a wider range of IT expertise.

The ensuing establishment of technical functions in organisations meant IT became an additional cost centre – established purely as a support function for the business, often underfunded, and lacking any interaction with business or customers. The department usually occupied the office's lowest-cost real estate, which added to the overall sense that IT wasn't considered that important.

Let's face it: it's challenging to support the overall organisational mission if you don't know what's *actually going on* in the business. But the IT department is core to, and a central business function of, any organisation in its own right. It's so much more than an enabler and supplier of technical support and maintenance.

Meanwhile, technology continues to evolve in all aspects of life and business. It has transformed our ways of working and living and created advances we've come to rely on and take for granted. That's the good – in fact, that's the great – thing about IT.

Yet the mindset and organisational structures around IT departments have often not kept pace with the rate of change. IT services have fundamentally changed over the last four decades, but the rate of change in IT service management hasn't kept pace.

Key message

Vicki Macdermid, TEDx speaker and creator of EQiLead Inc

Organisations will be at risk unless the crucial role of IT service management, including at the executive level, is recognised. The chief information/technology/data officer needs to have direct input into strategy at the very top level of the organisation, and IT professionals accorded recognition as key to success.

It's all about perception

Caricature of an IT geek

Picture the caricature of an IT nerd or geek. Do you identify with them? Whether you see yourself this way or not, you can probably easily come up with an image of someone who's more comfortable talking to a computer than to a person.

For example, are you the sort of person who wants to know – in depth – how the latest Tesla works, how technology is being used for remote medicine, or how the Mars mission will manage human waste (which is fascinating!)?

Traditionally, IT work attracts and employs people who have great technical skills, enjoy analysis, are often binary thinkers, and are excited by the latest breakthroughs and advances in technology. IT service management requires all those skills and more.

Is more the answer?

Many IT departments recognise the need for change. They want to be more efficient, more innovative and more valued. They want to partner with the business, be a trusted contributor, and to play a role in creating a great customer and employee experience. In other words, they want to be connected.

Instead, IT departments continue to use decades-old IT service management processes while continuing to look for more: more funding, more employees, more tools, more service providers, more transformations, more improvement initiatives – and the list continues.

What if 'more' doesn't mean what you think it means?

What if the central problem for IT departments is not the information – *or* the technology? What if it's the experience of IT service management when using and supporting the information and technology?

After all, there's more *information* available to us than we can possibly consume. There are more IT service management *technology* options than we need. Just ask anyone working in IT – Splunk, ServiceNow, SolarWinds, Jira, Zendesk (to name but a few) – all designed to help IT departments design and support IT services. But what about consideration of people and their experiences – the people using the information and technology, and the people in IT?

What you do matters

As an IT professional, everything we do (or do not do) has an impact. Day to day, we tend to focus on what we know best: resolving an incident, updating a knowledge article, creating a service transition framework, reporting on how our suppliers are meeting (or not meeting) service levels, and approving change requests. All of these are part of a well-trodden path of IT service management. But sometimes the question might occur to us: 'What value am I really adding?'

Fact: every action and task we perform (or do not perform) in IT service management has an impact on the experience of our users. This, in turn, affects our business outcomes and our organisation's mission. That's true regardless of whether the task is large or small. Everything we do impacts other humans, from resetting passwords to migrating data to the cloud. Ultimately, we should all contribute to the same goals that support business outcomes and our organisation's mission. Why?

- Because it keeps our business in business
- Because it's the best path to personal job satisfaction
- Because it shows we're team players
- Because it's how we earn the respect of the business and executive management
- Because it's our livelihood.

Let's stop here for a moment. You're probably starting to realise we are going to talk a lot about business outcomes and an organisation's mission – in fact, both of these concepts sit at the foundation of Humanising IT. So let's spend a little time ensuring we understand what each of these are. We've provided definitions and some examples below.

Definitions

- **Business outcome** 'Business outcomes are, in essence, the goals set by a company to measure the success or achievement of an internal or external process. These goals can also be labelled "desired outcomes" and are a useful way of helping staff to focus on achieving customer success.'[9]
- **Mission statement** 'Defines what line of business a company is in, and why it exists or what purpose it serves. Every company should have a precise statement of purpose that gets people excited about what the company does and motivates them to become part of the organization.'[10]

We mentioned in our introduction that, to aid in our learning, we have created a fictitious company called Fly First Airlines. We meet the staff, crew and passengers in later chapters. To help us further understand what a business outcome is, let's have a look at some of those at Fly First:

- On-time performance
- Consistent, timely and coordinated notifications of flight schedule and status changes to passengers and frontline staff
- Baggage arriving at the correct destination, in the assigned priority, at the scheduled date and time
- Accurate and optimised rosters available to manage crew operations
- All direct sales channels being available for bookings and payments.

On-time performance

On-time performance (commonly referred to as OTP) is considered one of the most important metrics used by airlines. An airline departure or arrival which is considered to be on time has a departure or arrival that occurs within 15 minutes of the scheduled time.[11]

And here is the airline's mission statement:

> To be the safest, most adored, most profitable, most sustainable and most recognised airline in the world.

So, whatever your reason, everything you do has an impact. And whether you decide to defer working on that incident (because it's low priority), reject a change request because a process step wasn't followed, or not update that knowledge article (because writing is a chore), sooner or later your decisions will impact your organisation's outcomes.

Therefore, the questions for IT service management professionals reading this book are:

- What are you doing, really?
- How does what you do support your business outcomes and your organisation's mission?

These are questions that often cannot be answered.

---

9   ServiceMuse. Achieving business outcomes with service excellence. https://servicemuse.com/business-outcomes-using-service/.

10   Corporate Finance Institute. What is a mission statement?
     https://corporatefinanceinstitute.com/resources/knowledge/strategy/mission-statement/.

11   OAG. What is on-time performance? https://www.oag.com/on-time-performance-airlines-airports.

A mop and the moon

Helping to put a man on the moon

It's 1962, and President John F. Kennedy is visiting the NASA Space Center. Mesmerised by the advanced technology of the era, he still takes the time to introduce himself to everyone he meets, including a janitor he sees mopping a floor.

'Hi, I'm Jack Kennedy. What are you doing, sir?'

The janitor pauses, puts down his mop, and says, 'Well, Mr President, I'm helping put a man on the moon.'

To most people, this janitor probably looked like he was simply cleaning a building. But in the larger story unfolding around him, he was helping to make history.

The story has become a legend, and for good reason: that janitor knew the value of his contribution. He could understand his role in the broader context of NASA's mission. He wasn't just mopping floors; he was contributing to the clearly stated outcomes of his organisation. It would be another seven years before NASA managed to achieve its mission.

We can only speculate whether that janitor was still mopping floors in 1969, when Neil A. Armstrong stepped onto the moon and announced it was 'one giant leap for mankind'.[12]

And here is NASA's mission statement today:

NASA explores the unknown in air and space, innovates for the benefit of humanity, and inspires the world through discovery.[13]

---

12   The Business Journals. What a NASA janitor can teach us about living a bigger life.
      https://www.bizjournals.com/bizjournals/how-to/growth-strategies/2014/12/what-a-nasa-janitor-can-teach-us.html.

13   NASA. Our missions and values. https://www.nasa.gov/careers/our-mission-and-values.

Your mission, should you choose to accept it

Let's take another look at IT service management. What are you really doing when you:

- Reset a password
- Provision a computer for a new user
- Connect a server to the network
- Install the latest software patches on your organisation's collaboration tools?

You may not be putting a man on the moon, but you could be doing something equally – or more – important. You might actually be:

- Assisting frantic staff at an airport check-in during a major weather disruption that has delayed 800 passengers travelling to see family and colleagues
- Helping busy nurses at a children's hospital to dispense life-saving medication
- Enabling a sizeable legal firm to submit crucial documents for a community class action
- Making sure anxious staff at a homeless shelter can contact their volunteers on Christmas Eve.

Let's start accepting that we all play a pivotal role in supporting the business outcomes and mission of our overall organisation. That can be our first step (or giant leap!) towards reorienting ourselves to the real world, stepping out of our specialised silos, and letting the world see us as we truly are and not as the caricatures forced upon us.

 Over to you

Can you describe your organisation's mission?

Can you identify three of your business outcomes?

Do you understand how your IT service management contributes to your business outcomes and organisation's mission?

What do you do, really?

Case study: Empathy and IT service management in a busy hospital

 *Ben Reid, director of ICT service delivery, Sydney local health district, Australia*

In 2019, before the Covid-19 pandemic, Ben Reid had a problem.

The IT service desk was meeting all its KPIs. Service desk analysts were responding promptly. User satisfaction rates were within agreed targets. On the surface, everything seemed to be working fine. So why was Ben hearing that the nurses were dissatisfied with IT? Ben asked his desktop team to spend one week away from their ticket queues from 3pm daily, and instead attend every ward in person. Every nursing station across two hospitals was visited. While waiting for the nurses to talk to members of the desktop team, a startling discovery was made: under the desks at the nurses' stations were piles of discarded IT devices, including tablets, keyboards and the occasional mouse. Each device was neatly labelled with the words 'Not working'.

The desktop team had no idea there were this many malfunctioning devices at the nurses' stations. As far as they knew, there wasn't a single service desk ticket about faulty devices anywhere in their backlog. Was this what the nurses were complaining about? And if so, why didn't they just log a ticket?

Ben took the time to observe the nurses at work. He discovered that nursing is a fast-paced and active job, and the nurses have little time to sit at a desk. After all, they are on shift in order to look after the health of patients, not to log IT issues.

Ben witnessed the way nurses spoke to and – most importantly – listened to their patients. For nurses, serving their patients is about empathising with a very human experience. He decided to follow their example and empathise with the people he himself was serving: the nurses on duty.

Through observation and discussion, Ben learned that whenever a device started malfunctioning, the nurses did whatever was necessary to keep meeting the needs of their patients: they found a working device and put the faulty one under the desk. They didn't have the time or motivation to contact the service desk. Consequently, the desktop team had no idea that there was a growing backlog of broken devices.

Eventually, the number of working devices dwindled, and frustration grew. If you asked a nurse at either hospital what they thought of IT, the answers were consistently negative. He realised that conventional best practice in IT service management doesn't consider the different circumstances and the different roles played by humans who use IT services.

Ben took his discoveries back to his team. They agreed that they needed to find a way to accommodate the speed and mobility of the nurses. Forcing them to adopt the existing service desk processes would hinder the entire mission of the hospitals, which was to provide 'excellence in healthcare' for patients and their families. It was equally clear that 'more' was not the answer: they had plenty of staff, plenty of funding, and plenty of equipment.

Member of Ben's team working with clinical staff

So the desktop team had to change the way they did even the most basic things. They started an experiment to see what would happen if they continued their daily visits to every ward in person for a month. On each visit, they checked in with the nurses on shift to see what IT problems they were having, and which devices needed attention. It turned out that the desktop team members were able to resolve many issues immediately, and for other issues, team members could log a ticket on behalf of the nurses.

Over the course of the month, the nurses came to love the visits by the desktop team, and their confidence in IT increased. The daily visits became a permanent KPI for the desktop team. Ben and his team continue to try innovative and yet simple strategies that place the human experience at the centre of all that they do to support the mission of the two hospitals.

Key learnings from the case study:

- IT service management statistics do not reflect the human experience
- Two simple acts can tell you volumes about how your IT services are being used: observation and listening
- Ultimately, it all comes down to empathising with the people you're serving.

Photos used with permission from the Sydney local health district, with thanks and gratitude to Ben Reid and his team.

Almost every human relies on IT service management

Think about this: almost every human on the planet depends on IT service management in one way or another. Whether it is a president addressing her nation, a hawker selling food in a Hong Kong laneway, or your local hardware store ordering inventory – all rely on IT service management in one way or another.

Now let's imagine if IT service management suddenly disappeared. What would happen? (The comedians among you may remark that everyone else would celebrate.)

Suddenly, there is no one to deal with that network outage, no one to coach a user through the installation of the latest organisational chat software, no one who can administer your customer database, or deliver real-time collaboration software that will allow your organisation to make good on the next cutting-edge technology.

Without a doubt, technological resources like computers, software and servers will – sooner or later – come to a crashing halt without the guidance of IT service management and IT professionals. It doesn't matter who or where a person is: almost every human relies on IT service management.

So can we do it any better?

You've heard the saying: 'If it ain't broke, don't fix it.' What's wrong with the way we've been doing IT? Well, nothing – and everything. For most industries, IT service management is a supply-and-demand game. Customers create the demand, and service providers try to meet or exceed customer expectations.

The disciplines of science and medicine are on a constant quest to find a better way, as is IT: a better way to create, record, track, transmit, communicate and work. This has led to better cameras, phones and networks. It's led to the World Wide Web, teleconferencing, smart devices and pacemakers. It's what makes remote work and matrixed teams possible. It's also what makes it possible to video-conference with grandparents on the other side of the world. And it's made air travel affordable, safer and more accessible.

But – and here's the but – these amazing advances that are pivotal to an organisation's mission, that can save and change a life, can revolutionise how we work and play, how we travel – all need to be supported, monitored, updated, integrated and even, occasionally, retired.

They need IT service management. And yet, IT service management continues to use decades-old processes based on potentially out-of-date 'best practice' guidelines that focus on supporting technology, not supporting the people we're here to serve and the people who are doing the serving. We think it's time to turn over a few rocks in the IT service management landscape and explore what's underneath.

Do not power down!

In 1822, Charles Babbage built the 'Difference Engine', generally considered to be the very first computer.

Personal computing has come a long way since Babbage messed around with vacuum tubes and rotating drums. For a start, we now have the internet. But even that has gone through a lot of changes since that fateful first networked message on 29 October 1969: a simple one-word transfer that managed to crash the entire system of networked servers on ARPANET.[14] There would be no World Wide Web for another 20 years, not until Tim Berners-Lee developed a proposal for a 'hypertext project'. Remarkably, Berners-Lee proposed that his web would be able to deliver both text and media, like graphics, video *and* sound.

He built his very first web server in a lab at CERN in 1989. The story goes that Berners-Lee took a careful and considered approach to IT service management. He taped a handwritten note to the server that read:[15]

This machine is a server. DO NOT POWER DOWN!

Most IT service management processes and tools feel a little like that handwritten note. Technology has become more and more powerful, but we're still relying on old-fashioned ways to manage it. Ideas and approaches are still in use that were designed before the advent of self-service, automation, artificial intelligence (AI) and modern architectures.

In our next chapter, we'll explore how to start modernising your IT service management.

Technology advances throughout history[16]

The telephone

The light bulb

The television

Personal computers

Global positioning system

The internet: ARPANET

GPS navigation

The digital camera

The web browser

Social media

The modern smartphone

---

14   That one word was 'login', by the way.

15   CERN. A short history of the Web. https://home.cern/science/computing/birth-web/short-history-web.

16   Lifewire. The 10 biggest technological advances since 1844.
      https://www.lifewire.com/biggest-technological-advances-since-1844-4588428.

Technology malfunctions that changed the course of history[17]

Hindenburg disaster

Leaded gasoline

Betamax

Google Glass

The Mars climate orbiter

Samsung Galaxy Note7 exploding phone batteries

Google+

The shuttle disasters

Penicillin

DDT

IT: It's complex

Technology can fail at so many points, it's almost a surprise that it works. The focus on simplicity for the user belies the complexity of the technology and the necessary support. Who hasn't heard people saying of the latest smartphone that 'It's so simple, a two-year-old can use it'? We all know IT is complex, but how much does the business understand that complexity?

Earlier, we reviewed the disconnect between the business and IT. We discussed sentiments that many IT professionals have heard from the business about IT: complicated, slow, expensive. But let's also celebrate how IT has transformed nearly every person on the planet – and herein lies the opportunity to transform how we deliver and support IT services: IT service management with a human focus.

It's about changing our culture and the way we work.

Recap

In this chapter, Mark Basham helped us explore and question the lack of IT service management culture in many organisations today. We also looked at challenges faced by IT departments – including how IT professionals feel they are perceived by the business. We further discussed a divide between IT departments and the business, and how this has contributed to the devaluing of IT service management that supports an organisation's business outcomes and mission.

Let's continue our journey in the next chapter, where we will delve into the transition from the conventional IT model to a human-centred design model. We will examine principles and practices from human-centred design and apply them to IT service management, including empathy and personas.

---

17   Tech malfunctions that changed the course of history.
      https://www.slashgear.com/825305/tech-malfunctions-that-changed-the-course-of-history/?utm_campaign=clip

2 Why do things go wrong in IT service management?

In this chapter, we will:

- Take a brief look at the traditional approach to, and history of, IT service management, and show how the 'one-size-fits-all' model doesn't work for every human (or even 'many humans')
- Show how the conventional focus for IT service management has been on technology, not the human experience
- Define the roles of customers and users
- Look at the proud tradition of the IT service desk
- Think about metrics, and how they are used to measure the success of IT services.

IT service management and the Model T?

IT service management is often seen as a sort of 'one-size-fits-all' approach with little customisation – or in the words of Henry Ford, referring to the mass production of Model T Fords:

Any customer can have a car painted any colour that he wants so long as it is black.

A totally utilitarian approach, with no customisation, not even for the paint colour. This resulted in maximising production output by creating certainty on exactly what was needed in each step of the process of manufacture. Incredible efficiencies resulted, utilising known and consistent processes. It reduced the training time for men on the line, ensured all tooling was utilised to the maximum and churned out thousands of vehicles of the same model.

Definition: One size fits all

Acceptable or used for a wide variety of purposes or circumstances; appealing or suitable to a variety of tastes.[18]

So, what's the connection between IT service management and the Ford Model T? Isn't this type of efficiency what we strive for in IT service management: known and consistent processes, everyone knowing their role, and tooling maximised? However, as we discuss in this chapter, Henry Ford realised that efficiencies alone do not equate to success – the experience of customers, as well as that of employees, challenges the concept of 'one-size-fits-all'.

---

18   Dictionary.com. https://www.dictionary.com/browse/one--size--fits--all

One size fits all – or does it?

1925 Ford Model T touring car

The Model T was the first mass-produced motor vehicle. Beginning production in 1908, Ford wanted to create a 'universal car' that was affordable, durable and easy to operate. These were worthy goals. The 'affordable' part meant Ford and his teams had to maximise efficiencies so they could pass their savings on to the consumer. At least, in theory they could.

In 1911, F. W. Taylor published a book called *The Principles of Scientific Management*. It suggested adopting a management style that came to be known as 'Taylorism', which uses scientific methods to analyse production processes in order to gain maximum efficiencies. Perfect!

Fordism

> The labor time needed to produce a Model T Ford fell from 12 h and 8 min in October 1913 to 1 h and 30 min 6 months later. Mass production thus conferred great competitive advantage but required workers to be organized and to work in specific ways, based around a separation of mental from manual work, extreme specialization of tasks, and a deep technical division of labor within the workplace. Workers typically perform simple, repetitive de-skilled tasks with very short job-task cycles (often defined in seconds) on the production line. The moving line delivers materials to them at speeds determined by management. Increases in labor productivity are achieved via increasing the line speed because of managerial decisions.
>
> R. Hudson[19]

19   R. Hudson. Fordism. In *International Encyclopedia of Human Geography*. Elsevier, 2009.
      https://www.sciencedirect.com/science/article/pii/B9780080449104001668.

Sticking doggedly to his goals meant Ford and his workers focused on creating production processes that were consistent and predictable, which resulted in incredible efficiencies and cost savings that could be passed on to the customer. Back then, a Model T retailed at a starting price of US$260. Not pocket money, but affordable enough for the average household.

The consistent procedures cut down on decision-making, reduced effort, minimised downtime and required the bare minimum of training to operate. All tooling was utilised to the maximum, and so were the workers. Many thousands of vehicles could be rolled off the production line in record time, for record savings.

Today, we call this approach to production 'Fordism'. Ford's approach to production was completely utilitarian. A 'one-size-fits-all' approach. There was no room for customisations. That's right: no one was going to push you to include optional 'add-ons'. No tinted windows or luxury upholstery or seat warmers. You couldn't even choose the colour of the paint.

But ... there was a catch.

Ford production line

When the Model T doesn't quite 'fit to a T'

The human experience was completely ignored. Obviously, customers who wanted a Model T that wasn't black were out of luck. *Every* Model T was black, at least during the heady heights of Fordism. Lovers of yellow, red, blue – really any other colour – weren't destined to have a fulfilling human experience with their one-size-fits-all black car.

And then there were the staff issues. Lots of staff issues. To paraphrase the article by R. Hudson in the callout, alienated workers performed repetitive tasks for hours (and days, and weeks, and ...) 'on an uninterrupted basis at a pace dictated by the speed of the line'. The length and timing of shifts were determined by the needs of the production machines, as dictated by managers who were ever committed to increasing efficiencies. As if speeding up production could only ever lead to benefits, not costs. No economies of scale for Fordists.

Workers, of course, began to despise their work. Working on the Ford production line was monotonous and repetitive. The Ford company prioritised efficiency over the very human experience of the job. The workers started to resist Fordism with industrial disputes and strikes. Nowadays we also know that repetitive work like this can result in accident and injury, which in a way is its own form of enforced downtime.

Eventually, Henry Ford realised he needed to change his production approach to maintain his customer base – and his staff – in the face of an increasingly competitive market.

What can IT service management learn from the Model T?

When IT service management began its life in the 1980s, the approach had many parallels with Fordism. IT service management was initially designed to ensure a uniform approach to managing infrastructure. Processes were systematic, documented, repeatable and 'known'. Nothing should be left to chance, said those early IT service managers. Everything should be designed so it could be applied consistently across different environments. It was as if IT service management itself was a machine.

At that time, most IT service management frameworks had two primary goals for managing technology: increase quality, and lower costs. Sounds familiar?

A formalised IT service management framework was a win for people who worked with and managed technology. It allowed for a standardised set of practices that any organisation could follow. We call standardised practices 'best practice'.

Who is 'best practice' really best for?

As we mentioned in Chapter 1, technology has changed and changed again. And it's changed us. The way we live and work has changed our approach to using, and our reliance on, technology. These changes mean that IT services, and how they are created, designed and supported, are fundamentally different from how they were way back in the 1980s.

Even the people (or should we say 'humans'?) using technology are different today. Thanks to the accessibility of devices and digital services, technology services aren't being used solely by professionals wearing ties and sitting in stuffy science labs on the campus of a major college. Technology is increasingly being used on the move, in all kinds of places, by people with and without computer science degrees.

The one-size-fits-all approach of Fordism couldn't even accommodate people who wanted a car in a different colour. What would it make of the diversity of users out there today, and the diversity of the IT professionals required to design and support the technology?

 Over to you

As an IT professional:

- What are the benefits of standardised practices?
- Where do you see disadvantages in the one-size-fits-all approach?
- Where do you see advantages in one-size-fits-all?

So how has IT service management evolved?

Many IT service management frameworks have evolved to meet new ways of designing and supporting IT services. But (isn't there always a 'but'?) the fundamental approach to IT service management is still the same as in the 1980s. The process of responding to a user issue or service request is almost identical to when IBM invented the term 'help desk' in the 1980s.

Conventional best practice in the IT service management model of an IT service desk design mandates a standard process for support or handling requests from users. The process usually assumes IT professionals have access to the right resources (including knowledge of the systems), that the issues can be resolved, and that requests can be fulfilled to the satisfaction of the users. So why do so many users find interacting with IT so challenging? There are many reasons, including:

- Long wait times
- Unclear instructions
- Complex problems that have no easy answer
- Proposed solutions that don't fix the issue, or inadequate workarounds
- Little to no understanding of the business impact of an incident.

Perceived challenges from users when contacting the IT service desk

The one-size-fits-all approach to incident management

Incident management is arguably one of the most utilised processes in IT service management. The process is designed to restore services as quickly as possible to ensure agreed levels of service are met.

And yet, reporting an incident has barely changed since the invention of the help desk. A user with an issue logs a ticket via the IT service desk. This process was based on the premise that the IT service desk should be the single point of contact for all users.

Who are all these users?

The term 'user' or 'authorised user' implies a homogenous group without consideration of differences, rarely considering the capability and needs of actual users. From the payroll manager requiring assistance to access a slow-performing payroll system to pay employees, to a newly onboarded graduate needing a new laptop, the request process is the same.

We do, however, concede that the design of IT service management does have a consideration that perhaps contradicts the above homogenous statement about users: the all-important VIPs. These users are considered too important to follow a process that ordinary users do.

Conceptually, this makes sense. It means there's one way forward: call (or text, message, email or chat with) the IT service desk. Users don't need to diagnose their problem and then find the correct contact details for that particular type of issue. The request process is the same, whoever the user may be.

So, what's the issue? The user is the issue. Or rather, the idea of 'the user' is the issue: the belief that there is one user, one homogenous group.

Let's play that out when we consider the following exercise.

 Over to you

Consider two or more people the same age and background as yourself – perhaps someone from your junior school who has taken a different career path in life. It will be best to consider someone who has a typical office job and someone who has a front-line job, such as a nurse, doctor, teacher or cleaner, or perhaps even a creative musician or artist. Consider for a moment what a typical working day might look like for each:

- How much of their working day do the different jobs require them to be at a desk?
- How many different people will each person interact with in a typical day?
- How would each person prefer to communicate with their colleagues?

Chances are, as an IT professional, you will have a more typical office job that requires you to be at a computer and desk for the majority of your working day.

Now consider:

- What might be the easiest way for people to contact you with an urgent issue?
- For the other people you have chosen, what might be the best way to contact them in a relatively urgent situation?

It's likely that the best way to contact someone with an office job is via email or perhaps even chat; however, someone working in a hospital is far more likely to answer their phone before responding to an email. How might you contact a performing artist in an urgent situation?

Office worker

Doctor

Musician

The point here is that we need to understand the different habits, behaviours and needs of our users. Just because someone is the same age and gender as another doesn't mean that they will engage with a service in the same way. Likewise, just because two users are of different ages, cultural backgrounds and genders doesn't mean that their needs are different. In order to understand what or who our users are, we need to research to understand.

In another example, consider two users who:

- Work for the same company
- Rely on IT to perform their roles
- Are tech-savvy

But one user has a computer issue directly impacting customers, and the other user doesn't.

User serving a customer who is unable to log in to the ticketing system to update passenger details

What is it we are saying? Humanising IT staunchly believes we have designed much of our IT service management with little regard for the different types of users in our environment.

And what else are we saying? Good question: in the next section we discuss different words used by the business and IT – where unknowingly we sometimes speak the same language but the words mean different things.

Human-centred design for IT service management

User working from home unable to update his timesheet

Let's talk about designing for humans

Traditionally, IT departments have been encouraged to deliver improvements and transformations as fast and efficiently as possible. Today, robots perform many of the most repetitive tasks on a vehicle assembly line. This is now becoming a strategic direction for IT service management: to automate processes and mundane tasks. There's one critical role that robots will never fulfil: the customer. And this is where Humanising IT integrates human-centred design into IT service management.

In the next chapter we will be learning about human-centred design in more detail. For now and for context, let's spend a few moments exploring some of its key concepts.

Human-centred design is about understanding people and creating innovative solutions based on their needs. It is also an approach to problem-solving that puts the customer first. It encourages designers to think outside traditional ways of thinking and to not feel constrained by 'best practice' considerations. It recognises that different people might have different needs and different uses – and services are designed around this premise.

Human-centred design is also an evidence-based approach where deep research forms part of the design process. It encourages people to fail fast, fail often and use rapid prototyping in the form of pen and paper, rope, sticky tape and elastic bands (whatever is at hand) – and often preliminary prototyping does not involve technology.

So, before diving into a solution mode aimed at service levels that we have assumed use the right metrics, in Humanising IT, we integrate human-centred design into IT service management, taking time to ensure that we are fixing the 'right' problem. Once we have clearly defined the problem, then (and only then) can we set about fixing the problem in the right way.

A key concept used in human-centred design is this: 'Designing for the right problem. Designing for the problem *right.*'

> It is about them and for them. The closer the end users' needs are analysed and answered, the more successful the adoption or purchase of a solution. You iterate until you get it right from a customer perspective. This the power of human-centred design.
>
> Olivier Delarue, UNHCR[20]

In Humanising IT, we not only advocate the principle of Olivier Delarue's quote, but we also ensure that the needs and motivations of the humans designing and supporting the technology are also considered – in other words, you!

And since we're on the subject of humans, let's talk about – well, talking. To humans.

Speaking different languages: business, IT and everybody else

One thing we didn't cover in our example of standardised incident management is this: what, exactly, is an incident?

For some people – mostly people outside IT departments – an incident is the same thing as an issue, which is the same thing as a problem, which might be the same thing as a 'glitch', an annoyance or a frustration. Any of these words might be used. So what do they mean?

If you are not an IT service management specialist – or even if you are – this may sound pedantic. However, it's necessary in IT to differentiate the terms so that the correct 'next step' is identified and the right people with the right skills are identified to receive the request. In other words: the right workflow is triggered, and the right resource is assigned.

Let's look at how the IT industry defines an incident and a problem:

Incident: an unplanned disruption of a service.

Problem: the underlying root cause of that disruption.

This can be compared to when we are sick – the symptoms are the incident and the disease is the root cause. Let's play this out because it's important. You have a headache, a runny nose and a sore throat – these are your symptoms. To find out what's really going on with your health, you may need to have an X-ray, a blood test or other specialist treatment to find the root cause of why you are unwell.

Can you see how we can express what some people would regard as the same thing in different ways? So it's no surprise that people in the business generally don't know the difference between incidents, issues, events, requests, problems – and anything else. It's because we haven't told them. The good news is that this gives us the opportunity to take the lead and start explaining ourselves so we can all speak the same language.

---

20   Oliver Delarue. Why use human-centered design for social impact.
      https://blog.movingworlds.org/an-introduction-to-human-centered-design/

Oh, and back to the definitions of incident and problem – here are the ones we'll be using in Humanising IT:

 Definitions

- **Incident** An instance of something happening; an unplanned event or occurrence that causes an unfavourable user or customer experience.
- **Problem** The underlying root cause of an incident (or multiple incidents)

Speaking different languages

Speaking of definitions, in the next section of this chapter we'll take a look at some of the most important ones we'll be using in this book.

 Over to you

- Does your IT department use a different language from the rest of the business?
- Does your IT department use a different language among vendors, teams, colleagues and peers?
- What do you think is more important to focus on, and why– incident or problem management?

Time to get the roles right: customers and users

IT service management aims to meet the needs of our customers. Or, should that be 'our users'? Or 'end users'? Or 'consumers'?

In Humanising IT, we define our key terms this way:

 Definitions

- **Customer** The person deriving value from the business services.
  Alternatively: the customer is the person who consumes the organisation's business services, deriving value from what the business does (e.g. a passenger on a plane or a patient in a hospital).

- **User** The person using the technology to deliver value to the customer.
  Alternatively: the user is the person in the business who delivers a service to the customer. They might be someone requesting an IT service or requiring IT support (e.g. a newly onboarded employee or frontline staff).

Ultimately, then, the services we're managing in IT service management are delivered to the *user* in the business, who in turn enables the *customer* to derive value. You could argue that the people in the business are *our* customers, and the people they're serving are *their* customers. To minimise confusion, we'll stick to 'users' (people in the business) and 'customers' (people who buy, or consume, from the organisation) as our definitions.

What defines a customer?

We could keep refining these definitions: a customer might also be anyone not directly using the service.

For example, for an airline, a passenger flying home is a customer, because she directly benefits from the organisation's service. She might have a child or partner at home who checks her estimated arrival time by accessing the airline's app. In Humanising IT, her child and partner are also customers because they benefit from one of the airline's services, even though they haven't flown on the airline's plane.

All design should be human-centred, it's as simple as that. And I mean human-centred, not 'user-centred' or 'user-friendly', because users are human beings after all. But, more importantly, because being human-centred is not just about your user. Human-centred design takes into account every single human being that your design decisions impact on.

Design Council[21]

---

21   Design Council. The seven tenets of human-centred design.
     https://www.designcouncil.org.uk/news-opinion/seven-tenets-human-centred-design.

Human-centred design for IT service management

What (and why) are we measuring?

Let's get back to discussing the typical landscape of IT service management and the ways in which it is measured. This will further demonstrate the fundamental problem of the traditional approach to IT service management.

'What gets measured gets managed.' This phrase, often (incorrectly) attributed to Peter Drucker,[22] has some truth to it. IT service management has created metrics to demonstrate how efficient and effective we are at delivering and supporting IT services. But how can we be sure we're measuring the right thing?

Let's take a look at a common measure: the volume of service desk tickets. Using any standard service desk software application, we can usually tell at a glance:

- The number of calls
- The average duration of calls
- The calls received each hour, day, week, month and year
- The average or total number of calls received by each analyst
- The number of calls resolved on first contact
- The number of calls escalated to other IT support staff.

We can't tell:

- How the user felt before, during or after the call to the service desk
- How the IT service desk analyst felt before, during or after the call with the user
- What the user is telling their colleagues and friends about the organisation's service desk
- What the analyst is telling their colleagues and friends about working on the service desk.

While most IT service desks automatically generate user feedback surveys, the response rate is notoriously low and questions can be leading (*confirmation bias* is something we'll discuss later in this book). Also, we usually wait until the request is resolved before asking for feedback. We rarely ask for feedback throughout the support process, resulting in missed opportunities to improve the user (and IT support staff) experience.

Is a high customer satisfaction rate a true reflection or not (when the response rate is as low as 3%)?

---

22 Peter Drucker (1909–2005) was one of the most widely known and influential thinkers on management, whose work continues to be used worldwide. He was a prolific author, and among the first (after Taylor and Fayol) to depict management as a distinct function and being a manager as a distinct responsibility. His writing showed real understanding of, and sympathy for, the difficulties and demands faced by managers. https://www.bl.uk/people/peter-drucker#:~:text=Peter%20Drucker%20(1909%2D2005),manager%20as%20 a%20distinct%20responsibility.

So, just like the customers of the Model T who wanted a car that wasn't black, or the bored factory workers on the production line, IT service management has traditionally ignored a critical component: the human experience of users and of the humans designing and supporting the service – meaning us.

What kind of experience are you delivering?

Shoot for the moon. Even if you miss, you'll land among the stars.

Norman Vincent Peale[23]

The quote by Norman Vincent Peale makes for excellent inspirational posters and encouraging memes on social media. But why are we using it in a book about IT service management? In Humanising IT, the moon is analogous to the lofty goal of creating a valuable human experience that can be felt and perceived by the people who benefit from the IT service.

The moon in perspective

To the astronaut on the way to the moon, or the sailor at sea, the stars are a means of navigation. But they're not the destination itself. Similarly, in IT service management, metrics such as availability, response time and mean time to restore are simply ways we measure the value we're creating. But they're not the value itself.

---

23   Gabe Gomes, the Masked Reader: Reaching For the Moon: The Autobiography of NASA Mathematician Katherine Johnson. https://www.orangeobserver.com/article/the-masked-reader-reaching-for-the-moon-the-autobiography-of-nasa-mathematician-katherine-johnson.

Over to you

Do your IT service management metrics measure experience or technology?

Can these metrics be related to how IT services help your organisation to achieve its business outcomes?

When efficiency drives inefficiency

There's another problem with measuring the wrong thing. Let's go back to the IT service desk. Efficiency metrics such as call volume or handling time can force service desk analysts to end a call without resolution, and sometimes with a sub-optimal workaround. This can be frustrating for users and exhausting for the service desk analysts.

In addition, these metrics can create inefficiencies downstream. For example, a service desk analyst provides users with a workaround that, later, is discovered no longer works. Either the service desk analyst will have to spend time and effort identifying all users who were informed of the workaround, or the users will contact the IT service desk to fix their now non-working workaround (and the latter is usually, if not always, the route taken).

The time it takes for the service desk analyst to follow up with the user or provide the new workaround could have been more wisely spent on tasks such as updating knowledge articles or closing tickets.

This traditional (and still widely adopted) approach to IT service management and metrics that does not consider a holistic view of the experience of both users and IT professionals provides further justification for why Humanising IT is needed.

Over to you

Can you identify at least three metrics that do little to add value for either the user or the IT professional?

What is one of the best IT service management metrics you have used or seen in use?

What is one of the worst IT service management metrics you have used or seen in use?

The IT service desk: more than a desk and more than a service

There are many capabilities, processes, practices or functions (or whatever we choose to call them) we could analyse to start answering the question posed at the beginning of this chapter: 'Why do things go wrong in IT service management?' We decided to explore the IT service desk – because, as you know, it's the face (and sometimes not a pretty one) of IT.

The IT service desk is the gateway to IT services for anyone outside the IT department. It's vitally important as a conduit and communication channel, and it's woefully underrated. One of the injustices of the IT service desk is in its name: it's incorrectly labelled as a 'desk', rather than 'support people' or any variation on the idea that humans are doing the work – not desks.

To use the conventional term 'IT service desk' ignores the fact that it is *humans* who are 'the desk'. Just as 'users' are often considered homogeneous, the service desk is not an inanimate object but rather individuals with knowledge, experience and desires as diverse as those of any user group. They are, in fact, users also – users of the system they operate in but have very little control over.

Swivel chair

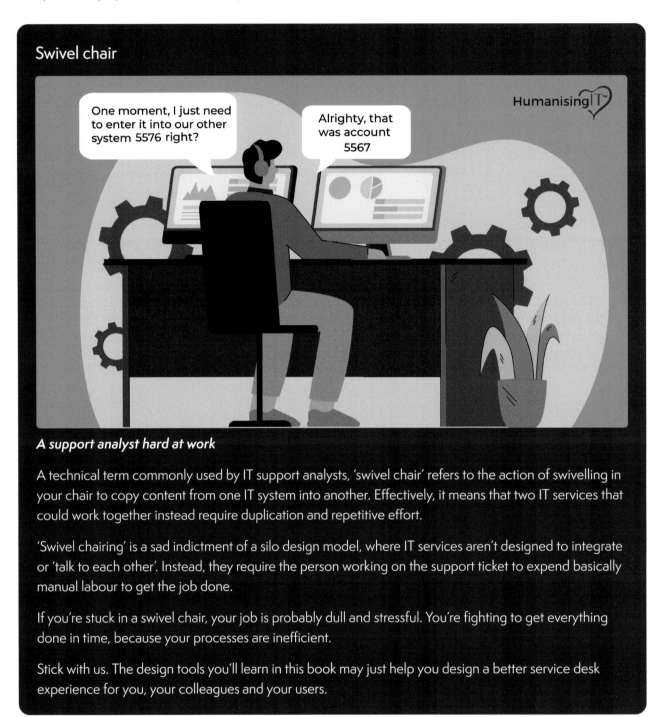

A support analyst hard at work

A technical term commonly used by IT support analysts, 'swivel chair' refers to the action of swivelling in your chair to copy content from one IT system into another. Effectively, it means that two IT services that could work together instead require duplication and repetitive effort.

'Swivel chairing' is a sad indictment of a silo design model, where IT services aren't designed to integrate or 'talk to each other'. Instead, they require the person working on the support ticket to expend basically manual labour to get the job done.

If you're stuck in a swivel chair, your job is probably dull and stressful. You're fighting to get everything done in time, because your processes are inefficient.

Stick with us. The design tools you'll learn in this book may just help you design a better service desk experience for you, your colleagues and your users.

As espoused by modern IT service management frameworks, a successful IT service desk focuses on user experience, where IT support professionals understand what the business does. Better customer experience and knowledge of the organisation enable better outcomes for users.

So, how do you, as an IT professional, acquire and maintain that knowledge? And how do you make sure the IT support analysts who have that knowledge are happy to continue working in those jobs, or in other jobs in your IT department?

Jeff Rumburg, in his article 'Metric of the month: Annual agent turnover', states that the average turnover in the industry is 'nearly 40% per year'. Further, 'in general, the more experienced the agent pool, the higher the first contact resolution rate and customer satisfaction will be'. [24]

A good IT service desk analyst is unlikely to spend years in the role. IT service desk roles are usually seen as a stepping stone to the dizzying heights of infrastructure or app support. But service desk roles themselves are often seen as less important than other roles, and are rarely described as a career destination.

So, from both an individual's perspective and the organisation's, is it worth investing the time and effort it needs to grow that knowledge if the service desk role is only ever transient?

The answer is: yes. Firstly, there are direct and indirect costs in recruiting, replacing, onboarding and offboarding employees in any workplace. Secondly, it means we get to provide a better human experience for the humans who work on our IT service desks. Not only is this good for our service desk analysts, but it's also good for everyone who comes into contact with them – which is everyone in the organisation.

So rather than treating the IT service desk and the humans who work there as the entry door to IT – striving to meet outdated KPIs such as call handling time – why not change the model and make the service desk the heart of IT, where all IT professionals (including the CIO) play an active role in providing services to users?

An IT professional rebooting

> It turns out that agent turnover is not only costly, it also has an adverse impact on service desk performance!
>
> Jeff Rumburg

---

24   Jeff Rumburg, HDI (Informa Tech). Metric of the month: Annual agent turnover.
      https://www.thinkhdi.com/library/supportworld/2018/metric-of-month-annual-agent-turnover.aspx.

Marco Bill-Peter, senior vice president of Customer Experience and Operations at Red Hat

Limiting the call duration is probably the worst idea I have ever heard – think about it. It means the employees are not able to get their work done, and the IT service desk analyst doesn't focus on getting these employees back to being productive. This is probably an easy calculation on how money is wasted internally.

Marco Bill-Peter

The Capability Maturity Model: reaching the unreachable

The following is a somewhat satirical and entertaining view of the Capability Maturity Model used by most IT departments to determine their IT service management maturity. Most IT professionals would be familiar with this model (along with the point of view expressed by the author).

We were unable to agree on a title for the article; Phillip Palmer, the author, a self-confessed and proudly articulated standards and best-practice nerd, preferred the title 'On being average'. We will let you decide.

The unreachable high of 5, or: On being average

Phillip Palmer, enterprise service orchestration evangelist

In 1986, the US Department of Defense released a development model known as the Capability Maturity Model. Its original purpose was to objectively assess the ability of government contractors' processes for implementing a contracted software project.

Capability maturity, as outlined by the model, related to the degree of formality and optimisation of processes. At one end of this spectrum was Level 1: a hellscape of ad-hoc, inefficient, unoptimised and costly processes. At the other end sat the mythical unicorn of maturity: Level 5 – the clean, pure, pristine and shining example of everything neat, tidy and *good* about process. The regal royalty of maturity looking down its nose at the slovenly, unkempt and downright barbaric Level 1.

'Ugh! How *vulgar* those Level 1s are! Just ... just *look* at them!' decries Level 5 in all its perfect optimised splendour.

Most maturity models, in the hands of consultants and other agencies, have been used to shaming you into feeling bad about your current situation. Like a teenage clothing line marketing campaign, or a personal hygiene product you've never heard of or wanted.

Ah, Level 5. Level 5 is perfect. Level 5 is everything you've ever wanted your process or operations or technology management or <insert topic of improvement here> to be. You should be like Level 5.

The best practice world has been flooded with various out-of-context-but-kinda-aligned-if-you-hold-it-up-to-the-light-in-a-certain-way-and-squint-real-good 'maturity models'. 'Baseline maturity assessments' have been the predominant blunt instrument of both major and freelance consulting firms.

You've never even seen a Level 5. You probably don't know anyone who has. You probably don't want to / could never / could never even understand how to be a Level 5.

It's OK to be 'average'.

You'll probably dominate your market space by being 'average' and just achieving Level 3. And *maybe* Level 4 is good enough to be 'great' against your competition.

As a self-described 'service management evangelist; standards and best practice nerd', I absolutely *love* standards and frameworks and models, but I despise having to do baseline assessments. The reasons are many, but the typical feeling is this:

You know you are rubbish at this. I know you are rubbish at this. Instead of taking 2 weeks to interview a bunch of people and put together a report to tell you what you already know (i.e. that you're rubbish) and then put together a multiple-page document that no one is ever going to read – and those who do will just argue against it to make them feel better about their situation – why don't we spend that money instead on putting in the fundamental things required to get you on a path to just be better than your competition?

Almost everyone I've ever assessed was sitting on a maturity level of about 1.5 to 2.25; this means that they had 'repeatable' processes (Level 2), but because they haven't made the effort to formalise them ('defined' – Level 3), their execution was a bit like a shotgun blast: generally pointing in the right direction, but the effects were all over the place, depending on who pulled the trigger.

What this means is that most of your competition is at the same level. What *that* means is that if you want to surpass them, you don't have to be the best at performing a process, you *just* need to be better than the competition. By being 'better', you'll become the best. See how it works?

In the end, getting to Level 3 is pretty much all that most organisations need to aim for. Unfortunately, Level 3 is a boring level to be at, because ultimately it boils down to four basic elements:

- Document what you do (say what you do)
- Perform to your documentation (do what you say)
- Record the performance as evidence (did you get what you hoped?)
- Continually improve based on your performance (did you improve? If so, let's make it better. If not, let's … make it better).

So there we have it. Excellence is overrated. *Exceptional comes from just focusing on being better.*

Key takeaway from this story

Philip's point of view is based on the premise that only processes are assessed when it comes to IT service management maturity levels. By contrast, the Humanising IT maturity model also assesses IT service management culture, because processes alone do not drive improvement.

Recap

In this chapter we examined Fordism and its similarities to traditional IT service management, and challenged the concept that 'one size fits all'. We began to explore what IT service management can learn from human-centred design and the traditional view of a 'user'. We defined two Humanising IT terms: 'users' and 'customers'. We explored the traditional approach to IT service management, and the importance of metrics that capture not just the performance of your services, but the experiences of the people using them. And finally, we discussed the importance of language between the business and IT, and ended the chapter with some self-reflection and satire by Phillip Palmer.

3   Introduction to human-centred design

In this chapter, we will:

- Reflect on and discuss the importance of starting design based on users (not on operational goals)
- Introduce some key concepts from human-centred design:
  - Empathy – one of the most crucial tools in the toolkit of every human-centred designer – including its history (yes, it has one!) and its shortcomings (there aren't many)
  - Personas
  - Proto-personas
  - Key user groups
  - Creativity, brainstorming and collaboration
  - Origins of human-centred design
- Take a detour into the DVF model (desirability, viability, feasibility) and witness how it can inform your design process, including:
  - How the DVF model can be used to build a collaborative design team for any solution
  - How to use the DVF model to collaborate with the most important people in your team: your users
  - A DVF checklist that you can use to build an awesome collaborative team.

Now we can talk about human-centred design

From this to this

Instead of beginning our IT service management design with operational goals, such as meeting KPIs and service level agreements, we need to start with the human experience of our users. What are their motivations, desires and context in the use of our IT services, and their objectives? Why, when, where and how do they need IT?

Human-centred design is a creative problem-solving process that begins with understanding human needs and ends with innovative solutions to address those needs.

Human-centred design principles are used in fields such as customer experience, user experience and digital design. And while there are a multitude of confusing and overlapping terms that get thrown around in the human-centred design space, when you get down to it, it's fundamentally about understanding people (their needs, constraints, contexts, behaviours and wants) in order to build empathy and make sure we design solutions to cater to the people who use our services.

When we talk about 'design' in this way, we are not talking about styling or aesthetics. There is no photoshopping here. Instead, 'design' in human-centred design is the methodology used to capture human needs, and to define solutions, processes and outcomes to respond to the human experience and ultimately achieve your organisation's mission.[25]

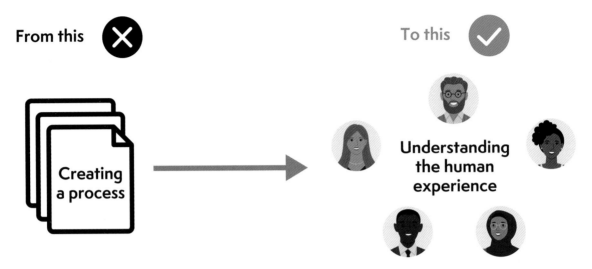

Figure 3 From working in isolation (to create a process) to working together (to understand the human experience)

In Humanising IT, we integrate 'human-centred' into IT service management, so that we start from a position of understanding the users (Figure 3). But before we go any further, we need to take a long, hard look at ourselves – and other people – using one of the most powerful tools human-centred design has to offer: *empathy*.

Empathy

Start with people, not processes

In Chapter 2 we explored the fact that most, if not all, IT organisations have designed their IT service management processes with little regard for the different types of users in their environment. Do you recall the office worker, doctor and musician analogy in Chapter 2?

What do you really know about your users? For example:

- What are their motivations, desires, contexts and circumstances?
- What are their objectives?
- Why, when, where and how do they need IT?

Human-centred design is built on the foundational belief that you need to understand the humans who are experiencing the problem before you can design a solution to solve that problem. So, how do you do that?

It all begins with empathy

Now, we're going to get to grips with this fundamental human-centred tool.

---

25   What the hell is human centered design? https://yellcreative.com/what-is-human-centred-design/

Definition: Empathy

'The action of understanding, being aware of, being sensitive to and vicariously experiencing the feelings, thoughts and experience of another of either the past or present without having the feelings, thoughts and experience fully communicated in an objectively explicit manner.'[26]

What's the big deal about empathy?

Empathy is at the very core of what human-centred design does, and we use this tool in Humanising IT:

- Empathy helps us walk in the shoes of the humans for whom we're designing and supporting services
- Empathy lets us build a human connection between us and our users
- Empathy means we get to experience what it's like to consume our IT services – without self-defensiveness, fear, judgement or assumption
- Empathy allows us to step out of our own predefined and biased beliefs about our IT services.

Empathy is a respectful understanding of what others are experiencing. Instead of offering empathy, we often have a strong urge to give advice or reassurance and to explain our own position or feelings. Empathy, however, calls upon us to empty our mind and listen to others with our whole being.

Marshall Rosenberg[27]

If you only remember one thing from this section, remember this: the human-centred design process begins with empathy, not processes or assumptions of what good looks like. It doesn't rush to find a solution in order to 'make the problem go away'. It doesn't charge ahead to meet project timelines and budgets. And it doesn't design services to achieve service level agreements. No: instead, empathy emphasises *understanding*.

As the quote from Marshall Rosenberg implies, you can't empathise with someone and judge them. Empathy asks us to listen, observe and understand. Empathy will also make it easier for you to collaborate with the users who are seeking a solution to their (very specific) problem. Empathising enables us to immerse ourselves in the worlds of other people, which allows us to gain insights into their real needs, not the needs we assume they have.

The following case study provides an excellent story about the power of empathy.

---

26   Merriam-Webster dictionary. https://www.merriam-webster.com/dictionary/empathy.

27   Marshall Rosenberg (2003). *NonViolent Communication: A Language of Life*. PuddleDancer Press.

Case study: Empathy and the squishy gripper

We already know how people brush their teeth, right? Or do we?

Have you ever looked at a kids' toothbrush? Maybe you have if you happen to be checking whether someone's brushed their teeth before bed. And, if you're paying attention, you may have noticed that children's toothbrushes are different from adult versions. They're not just smaller – they're actually shaped differently, too.

The humble toothbrush is a surprisingly ancient technology.[28] Those first 'chewsticks' started appearing around 3000 BC. Back then, they were no more than a thin twig that people rubbed against their teeth. Effective and environmentally sound, if not exactly a sophisticated approach to oral hygiene.

Then, in the 15th century in China, a revolution occurred. People started attaching coarse boar hair to a bone or bamboo handle, more closely approximating to the toothbrush we know today.

It wasn't until 1780 that toothbrushes became a mass-produced product, thanks to William Addis. But it took until 1938 for people to start replacing boar hair with nylon bristles. And just a year after that, the Swiss invented the electric toothbrush. Teeth were on a sparkling roll!

A child brushing her teeth

So, in 1996, when Oral B approached the design firm IDEO to help it design a new toothbrush for kids, the first thing the IDEO team did was sit down and ... watch a bunch of kids brush their teeth.[29] Why?

You probably guessed the answer: empathy! Most people probably thought they already knew how kids brushed their teeth – just like adults brushed their teeth, only smaller and closer to the floor. So the logical conclusion was that to develop a new kids' toothbrush, they should make an adult toothbrush, only smaller, to meet the smaller sizes of children. Right?

Wrong. As it turns out, IDEO discovered that the way kids hold a toothbrush is totally different from the way adults do it. Go figure! As adults, we tend to have greater dexterity in our hands, and we use our fingers to manipulate the toothbrush with finer movements than kids can manage. Kids, on the other hand, grab the toothbrush in their fists.

IDEO realised kids needed a different kind of toothbrush so they could grip it. A smaller toothbrush wasn't going to be the solution. They learned that through simple, careful observation. That one simple insight led to a totally new style of toothbrush: the squishy gripper.

That's right: using empathy and observing kids brushing their teeth entirely changed the kids' toothbrush space.

---

28 Library of Congress. Who invented the toothbrush and when was it invented?
    https://www.loc.gov/everyday-mysteries/item/who-invented-the-toothbrush-and-when-was-it-invented/.

29 Great Learning. How Oral B designed the best-selling kid's toothbrush using design thinking?
    https://www.mygreatlearning.com/blog/how-oral-b-designed-a-best-selling-kids-toothbrush/.

IDEO

IDEO is recognised for its innovation and promoting the use of human-centred design in the modern world. If you are learning about human-centred design, we believe you should know about this world-renowned company and its founder, David Kelley. The extract below provides a solid overview of both.

IDEO is one of the most innovative and award-winning design firms in the world. They're like the secret weapon of innovation for companies like Microsoft, Hewlett-Packard, Pepsi, and Samsung, in large part, due to their focus on human-centred design.

Over the last few decades, they've designed hundreds of products, like the first computer mouse for Apple in 1980, the Palm Pilot in 1998, a school system in Peru, and the 25-foot mechanical whale used in the movie Free Willy, just to name a few.

But perhaps the most interesting thing about IDEO is that founder David Kelley doesn't consider them to be experts in any specific industry or vertical. He says, 'We're kind of experts on the process of how you design stuff.'

You could hire them [IDEO teams] to design a vending machine, an app, a mattress or a space shuttle, and it would all be the same to them. [...]

IDEO designers trust that as long as they stay connected to the behaviours and needs of the people they're designing for; their ideas will evolve into the right solution. In other words, they let the end user tell them what they need to focus on building. David Kelley said, 'If you want to improve a piece of software all you have to do is watch people using it and see when they grimace, and then you can fix that.'

Sometimes the best ideas are so obviously staring us in the face that we miss them. We can't see them because we're looking at things from the outside in, instead of looking at things through the eyes of the end user.

That's why the folks at IDEO strategically put users at the core of everything they do – a process they refer to as human-centred design.

UserTesting[30]

How to be empathic: A user guide

If empathy is beginning to sound like a miracle ingredient that you don't have at hand, or fear you will never have, don't panic. We have some practical tools in this chapter and the following chapters that will put some structure around the simple instruction to 'listen and learn'.

We learned that the IDEO designers behind the squishy gripper kids' toothbrush had a simple tenet for their research: *empathy for the user*. They believed that the key to figuring out what humans genuinely want lies in doing two things:

- Putting yourself in the shoes of the user
- Observing user behaviour.

---

30   UserTesting. IDEO's human centered design process: How to make things people love.
      https://www.usertesting.com/blog/how-ideo-uses-customer-insights-to-design-innovative-products-users-love.

There are numerous designs and methods for designing with empathy, but broadly speaking the five steps outlined below are the most common approaches used.

- **Step 1** Understand the human experience and needs of the target audience
- **Step 2** Generate a wide variety of ideas to solve the problem of the human experience, which should involve the people whose problem you are solving
- **Step 3** Translate some of these ideas into prototypes
- **Step 4** Share these prototypes with the people you are designing for to gather feedback
- **Step 5** Build the chosen solution for release.

When an IT team designs with empathy, the starting place is knowledge of the human experience of people using your services. As we learned in Chapter 2, these are your *users*, and this ultimately helps the team to support business outcomes for customers and achieve your organisation's mission.

Let's recap these key definitions we use in Humanising IT.

 Definitions

- **Customer** The person deriving value from the business services.
  Alternatively: the customer is the person who consumes the organisation's business services, deriving value from what the business does (e.g. a passenger on a plane or a patient in a hospital).
- **User** The person using the technology to deliver value to the customer.
  Alternatively: the user is the person in the business who delivers a service to the customer. They might be someone requesting an IT service or requiring IT support (e.g. a newly onboarded employee or frontline staff).

Problem in chair not in computer (PICNIC)

Human-centred design for IT service management

How you can think like the innovators at IDEO

Don't ask, observe

The key to empathy is to remove any assumptions and focus solely on what the person is thinking, feeling and experiencing.

Here's a shocking fact: just asking people what they think, feel or do isn't enough. What people say they do and what they actually do can be different things. Just like what they say they want and what they'll actually use can be different.

Although the validity of the following quote (regularly attributed to Henry Ford but unverified) is sometimes perceived as folklore, it provides a perfect analogy to think like the innovators of IDEO:

> If I had asked my customers what they wanted, they would have said a faster horse.
>
> Henry Ford

Faster horses or arriving faster?

Henry Ford had a point. If he'd asked his customers what they wanted, they might have said a faster horse. But observation allows us to realise that what they're actually trying to achieve is 'to get from here to there' as efficiently as possible. The way they *think* they can achieve that is with a faster version of what they've always used.

But faster horses aren't always the answer. The inventors of cars knew that. You need to observe your users in their environments, you need to observe without judgement or assumption, and you need to know what problem needs to be solved (not the solution).

If you asked your users what they wanted when they contact the IT service desk, they would probably say, 'I just want my issue fixed.'

But is that what they *really* want? What they probably want is to get back to being productive. Not to have the issue in the first place. Feel they are being listened to. Be spoken to in a respectful, non-judgemental manner. To have the opportunity to learn about the issue so if it occurs again, they might be able to fix it themselves.

You see, it's much more than just 'fixing the issue'. Once you realise this, you can start to design more creative solutions than a traditional IT break/fix response.

Later, we'll talk about some specific research tools you can use when practising empathy (and we'll also explore the concept of break/fix in detail). For now, let's keep discussing empathy.

> Service design is a collaborative process for researching, envisaging and then orchestrating experiences that happen over time and multiple touch points.
>
> Oliver King[31]

 Over to you

Describe two priorities that the Oral B designers used in developing empathy for the human experience.

Who are your users, and what are their motivations, context, needs and constraints when using IT services?

What concrete action can you perform to gain deeper empathy for your users' human experience?

Empathy: The miracle ingredient – or is it?

By now, you're probably thinking, 'Wow – as well as being that miracle ingredient, empathy sounds like something that will supercharge everything I do from here on out! How come it's not used all the time?'

You might be surprised to hear that there can be drawbacks to using empathy as a research tool. For one thing, empathy takes time and patience. You can't program empathy for 3:00pm to 3:30pm on a Thursday and assume you can design a perfect service.

You need to practise empathy and learn how to interpret what you're observing. You also need to be sure you're observing the kind of users you're designing your services for.

Finally, it might be difficult to convince your management and colleagues of the value of empathy. When this happens, remember to share the story of Oral B's toothbrush for kids!

This phase of the design process is creative, messy and occasionally confrontational. To someone without much experience, it can feel chaotic, especially to people new in this field who are accustomed to following best-practice IT service management processes. Stick with it, though. You'll be amazed at some of the discoveries you can make.

---

31   Oliver King: What is service design? *Touchpoint, The Journal of Service Design April 2009.*
      https://www.parlament.gv.at/ENGL/ZUSD/PDF/What_is_Service_Design.pdf.

It's that time again

Once you've explored all options from multiple perspectives and sources, you're ready to start the next phase in human-centred design and start narrowing down the possible solutions.

Note: We will be learning more about the different phases in human-centred design in our next chapter.

Observation and empathy: An IT case study

Here's a case study I wrote that uses empathy in an IT setting. It was one of those 'A-ha!' moments that happened during the course of my studies.

I learned that when you get the chance to observe your users and empathise with them, you need to pay careful attention to their actions and emotions (and in this case the physical artefacts in their environment), and listen. Because often, you will discover that there are things that aren't being recorded or talked about. You know: non-technical things. These things can have the biggest impact on the user's experience of an IT service.

This was definitely the case for Bob[32] the baggage handler when he received his new iPad!

Bob's iPad example demonstrates that by simply observing how users make use of a product in a real-life work situation, you can potentially (and more likely) design a better human experience for them. And remember, in Humanising IT we also consider the experiences of IT professionals who design and support the technology – meaning you.

---

32   The name of the person in this case study has not been disclosed.

An IT case study in empathy: An iPad for lunch?

While I was researching for an assignment, I spent time on-site observing the ground crew of a major airline.

An iPad for lunch?

One day, I was visiting Bob, a long-serving and devoted employee in baggage handling. As it happened, Bob had recently received an iPad from IT.

'This device is great! It really helps with my work, Kat,' he told me. After proudly showing off his newest acquisition, Bob carefully slipped the iPad into a large sandwich bag on his desk. Spotting my confusion, he explained, 'It rains a lot in this part of the world. The sandwich bag protects my iPad from getting wet.'

You see, Bob had to work outdoors most of the day, handling baggage – something that we in the IT department hadn't really considered. The iPad was great, but he had no way to protect the technology that was supposed to make his job easier. So he'd come up with a creative – and cost-effective – solution of his own.

In IT, we tend to ask, 'What do you want?'

First, we assume people like Bob know the latest technology offerings or can intuit a better way to work. What we're *not* doing is spending time with Bob, observing his work and activity out on the tarmac and under the terminal. We're not speculating how he works or how technology can help automate the tasks he has to do – we've no doubt assumed many things.

By asking Bob to show me where he works, what he does prior to work, how he tracks baggage, how and when he records his time, identifies risks, reports incidents and so on, I was able to make some startling insights.

One of the other things I noticed was that Bob and his team liked to print documents. When I asked Bob why there was so much paper on his desk, he replied that the font on the baggage tracking software was too small to read. No one had showed him or his colleagues how to increase and zoom the application.

Were we in IT designing technology that suited his way of working? Was it methodical, easy to use, accessible and necessary? Did Bob need 20 buttons on his time-tracking software just to record his shift? Did he want an iPad with a waterproof cover?

A hard-working person like Bob doesn't like to complain or make a fuss. They're focused on the job at hand. Just like we should be.

But how can you be sure you're providing the best and most workable solutions for the experience that Bob is having in his workplace? How can we develop innovative solutions for the work experience he could be having?

One final note: as you look at Bob's desk, take a look at his creative solution for a 'deluxe' monitor stand (two reams of paper versus one).

Personas

Do we really know our users?

One of the activities (and skills) that is distinctly lacking in IT service management is taking into consideration the different types of users, along with their motivations, constraints and pain points when using our services.

In Chapter 2 we questioned how well we knew our users, and compared the life styles of an office worker, doctor and musician. We felt that this was a great example to show how 'on paper' users may seem the same (similar ages and backgrounds) – after all, aren't they just people who use IT?

You probably already knew this, but most IT organisations continue to design IT service management with little regard for the different users of their services (except, of course, that all-important VIP user). As you are learning, Humanising IT integrates the techniques used in human-centred design. The first of these is empathy, and in this section, we explore *personas*.

What are personas? Great question. Personas are used to represent a group of customers and summarise the key characteristics of one or more individuals who exhibit similar attitudes, goals and behaviours in relation to using a service.

 Definition: Persona

'Personas are fictional characters, which you create based upon your research in order to represent the different user types that might use your service, product, site or brand in a similar way. Creating personas helps the designer to understand users' needs, experiences, behaviors and goals.'[33]

Personas are used extensively in many (if not most) industries as profiling for customers. The big tech brands we are all familiar with, such as Apple, Google and Microsoft, invest heavily in crafting the technique and the use of personas. Even the not-so-big brands are now adopting the use of personas in the design of services for their customers. That's because personas allow companies (including those big tech companies) to know:

- Their users
- Who they are
- What they like
- What their pain points are
- The real problem that needs to be solved.

The design and use of personas is not particularly new, and they have been used as an effective design tool for decades. In many instances, experiences are designed based on personas. For example, how you buy your groceries online or travel on an aircraft – invariably you have matched a persona that a digital or marketing team has created. These teams do this to ensure that services match their customers' desires, capabilities and motivations, and ultimately so that customers have a good or great experience (not all experiences are designed to be great).

---

33   Interaction Design Foundation. What are Personas? https://www.interaction-design.org/literature/topics/personas.

For example, these digital and marketing professionals have identified that an elderly gentleman (persona) who travels very infrequently requires a different service experience than a businesswoman (persona) who travels the globe regularly (and in style).

A good, effective persona:

- Expresses and focuses on the major needs as well as expectations of one of your most important user groups
- Embodies one of the major user groups of your service
- Provides a clear picture of your users' expectations and how they are likely to use your service
- Aids in identifying how they are likely (or not likely) to use your service
- Represents real people, incorporating their goals, delights and background.

 Key message

There are many elements that can be incorporated into personas, and the ones listed above are the most common – including goals, delights and background.

There is a raft of examples freely available online, and we encourage you to spend some time to ensure a good understanding of the different elements that can be used within a persona.

Personas are great – but ...

Although personas are used extensively in human-centred design and are foundational to the design process, it's important to be aware of some disadvantages:

- Personas take time and effort to get right – in other words, they are costly to create
- Personas can be hard to sell to your stakeholders – this is especially true in an IT organisation where there is a low level of customer-centric maturity
- Creating personas requires the right skills, and isn't something that you can just start doing. Training and coaching in the methods and techniques of how to create a persona are required.

So, although the concept of personas is used extensively in other fields, they are not used particularly extensively by IT professionals when designing IT services for our users. Humanising IT incorporates personas, and, like human-centred design, personas are foundational in our approach to IT service management and Humanising IT.

The 'persona' as a mask

The word 'persona' is derived from the Latin *persōna*, meaning 'mask'. In psychology, the concept of the persona was developed by Swiss psychologist Carl Jung to refer to the 'mask' that's used to hide the true nature of a person (called the *anima*).[34]

---

34   Dictionary.com. https://www.dictionary.com/browse/persona.

Over to you

We mentioned above that not all experiences need to be great, and sometimes good is good enough (when you want something to be done quickly and seamlessly). Sometimes services that are easy to use are better than ones that offer a 'unique or incredible experience'.

Can you identify three reasons why human-centred designers don't always design a great service experience?

Can you think of needing to complete something where you didn't want a 'great service'?

Why are personas so important to the design process?

The most important goal of personas is to create understanding and [here's that very important word, with our italics] *empathy* with the end user.

If you want to design a successful service for people, first of all you need to understand them. Designing for everyone results in an unfocused goal that will dehumanise the profile of future users. The personas method allows you to draw not just a profile about gender and age, but to dig into the psychology of the imagined character in their interaction with the product.

KeepItUsable[35]

Personas help designers find the answer to one of their most important questions: 'Who are we designing for?'

We'll now take another look at our fictitious company, Fly First Airlines. (You may recall we explored the airline's business outcomes and mission in Chapter 1.)

We'll delve deep into the workings, challenges and successes of Fly First Airlines in Chapter 6 – but to help us understand personas, and for context, we have provided a snippet about the airline below where we also meet an employee (well, a persona of the airline). We do hope you enjoy our storytelling approach to Humanising IT and the importance of considering not only the human experience of our users but also that of the IT professionals who design and support the technology.

Fly First Airlines proudly employs over 20,000 people from a diverse range of backgrounds, skills and cultures. Its headquarters are in Melbourne, Australia. The frontline staff of the airline play a pivotal role in ensuring passengers have a safe and enjoyable journey. Carmen (our persona) is the airport supervisor at Sydney, Australia – one of the airline's busiest airports.

---

35   Keep It Usable. Personas: Why is it important to understand your users?
      https://www.keepitusable.com/blog/personas-why-is-it-important-to-understand-your-users/.

An example of a persona created for frontline workers at our fictitious company, Fly First Airlines

Carmen's job is varied and busy. She has strong leadership qualities, tact, initiative, good judgement and an ability to get along with others. She has a good understanding of the needs and concerns of the various users of the airport, including aircraft operators, concessionaires and the general public.

> Personas provide direction for making the right decision in the design of products and services.
>
> David Kelley[36]

Proto-personas

Proto-personas are another technique used in human-centred design to better understand users. They represent a limited snapshot and do not require in-depth research. They are made on an ad-hoc basis, and have low fidelity.

---

36   David M. Kelley is an American businessman, entrepreneur, designer, engineer and teacher. He is the founder of the design firm IDEO and a professor at Stanford University.

Definition: Proto-persona

'... a lightweight form of ad-hoc personas created with no new research. They catalogue the team's existing knowledge (or best guesses) of who their users are and what they want.'[37]

Proto-personas versus personas

As we learned in the previous section, a persona is the result of a much more involved process. It is based on in-depth research; it has a longer timeline of usability, and high fidelity to its real-world context.

A proto-persona, like a persona, would typically include users' goals, needs, pain points and delights.

Key characteristics of personas:

- Heavily researched representation of the target audience
- Detailed
- Professionally finished with specialised software used to create them.

Key characteristics of proto-personas:

- Utilises existing research or material; no new research is performed
- Ad hoc
- Low fidelity – often sketched, and often created during a brainstorming session.

 Over to you

Can you identify three proto-personas that contact your IT service desk?

Now that you have identified these proto-personas, are you able to empathise with how they interact with your IT service desk?

---

37   Nielsen Norman Group. 3 persona types: Lightweight, qualitative, and statistical. https://www.nngroup.com/articles/persona-types/.

Table 1 Four examples of proto-personas

Luis – application support	Daria – airport check-in agent	April – passenger	Mandy – head pilot
Luis supports most of the critical applications used by airport staff. He has been at the airline for 3 years. He gets frustrated by IT support teams passing tickets to other support teams (known as 'ticket bouncing') and taking little responsibility for the IT issue. Luis has tried numerous times to educate not only his team but all IT support teams about the impact of ticket bouncing on users, but he has had little success. His goal is to create a great working environment for everyone.	Daria has been at the airline more years than she cares to count. Daria is a hands-on problem-solver. She is not very tech-savvy and has a fractured relationship with IT. Due to the advances in technology and the adoption of many new IT systems at the airport, Daria's job relies heavily on IT. Daria's goal is to ensure passengers move through the airport smoothly.	A loyal Fly First customer, April travels regularly for work and leisure. April is prepared to pay extra for great service and will only fly business class. April has been known to post negative reviews on social media if her flight is delayed or she experiences poor service before, during or after a flight. April's goal is to get to her destination with as little hassle as possible – in style!	Mandy is the head pilot at Fly First Airlines – she loves flying aircraft. Mandy relies heavily on IT. She is very tech-savvy and feels she knows more about aircraft applications than the IT staff do. Mandy's goal is to ensure she gets her passengers safely to their destination so she can return home to her partner and children.

Key user groups

Another human-centred design technique is to create key user groups. This technique is useful if budget or time prevents the creation of a persona, and can also be used as the starting point for creating proto-personas and personas.

 Definition: Key user group

A key user group is a set of people who have similar interests, goals or concerns.

Examples of key user groups

Lucy, 30: 'I look for the cheapest route.'

Patrick, 62: 'I want to feel cosy and comfortable.'

Caroline, 37: 'My priority is that my family is safe.'

 **Over to you**

Can you explain the differences between a persona, proto-persona and key user group?

Which concept would you most likely use in the design of your IT service management, and why?

Creativity, brainstorming and collaboration

Before we go any further, let's take a look at some of the key concepts and principles of human-centred design.

Every human is creative

Human-centred design is a creative process. What, me – *creative*? But I work in IT! I hear you. But I believe – and human-centred design believes – that every human is creative, and problem-solving is an inherently creative process.

Could you really come up with the Oral B squishy gripper without being creative? Similarly, could you organise your website content, develop a new incident management tool or build an app without creativity? Could you write a user manual or uncover a workaround if you weren't, somewhere deep down, a creative thinker?

Could you cook a meal without some amount of creative thinking? Even if you're following a recipe, some of what you're doing requires you to interpret what you read and apply it in your own kitchen. That's creative!

Creative thinking can include both divergent and convergent thinking (we cover these concepts in Chapter 5). It's creative to open yourself up to new ideas. But it's also creative to eliminate the unnecessary or unworkable ideas, and home in on what could work in a given situation.

So, yes, that means even IT service management professionals are creative human beings.

Brainstorm for quantity, not quality

Brainstorming is a fundamental human-centred design tool. During brainstorming, you're using divergent thinking.

If you've never brainstormed before, just remember this: no idea is a bad idea. The emphasis in brainstorming is on generating a rich *quantity of ideas*, not *quality ideas*. The greater the variety of ideas you come up with, the more likely it is that you'll reach the very best solution for the specific problem you're addressing. No idea is a bad idea, because even a bad idea can inspire a great one.

Remember, when brainstorming:

- Don't judge or criticise other people's ideas
- Encourage everyone to come up with the craziest, wackiest and weirdest ideas they can
- Build on other people's ideas and see how far you can extend, challenge or dismiss them
- But, importantly, set a timer – otherwise you might never stop brainstorming!

Collaborate and communicate

Human-centred designers collaborate. They collaborate with stakeholders (which could mean anyone from customers, users and suppliers, to other experts within and outside of the IT department). Collectively, these collaborative groups work together to ensure an organisation can deliver services or products that support its business outcomes and achieve its mission.

The origins of human-centred design

Human-centred design is rapidly gaining popularity in various industries across the globe. Interested learners may ask: where did human-centred design come from?

While elements of what we call 'human-centred design thinking' have long been documented throughout human history, human-centred design as we know it today started to evolve during the 20th century, and can largely be attributed to people in Silicon Valley, Stanford University and IDEO.

 Definition: Participatory design

An approach to design that invites all stakeholders (e.g. customers, employees, partners, citizens, consumers) into the design process as a means of better understanding, meeting and sometimes pre-empting their needs.[38]

---

38   Olga Elizarova and Kimberly Dowd (2017). Participatory design in practice.
       https://uxmag.com/articles/participatory-design-in-practice.

In ancient Greece, philosophers such as Plato were known to have used a form of participatory design in the solution of pressing political and philosophical problems of his day.

Plato was known to use human-centred design

The DVF model: Give 'em what they want?

Let's get something clear: human-centred design isn't *just* about giving everyone what they want. You can't deliver everything your customer wants. If you tried, you'd probably:

- Expend your budget very quickly
- Design services that are too expensive for people to afford, or for you to support
- Develop a catalogue of services that appeals to only a handful of people
- Provide services that aren't aligned with the organisation's business outcomes or mission.

So, how do you come up with a solution that your users want, that you can afford, and that you have the capability to build or provide? That's where the DVF model can be used (see Figure 4).

A balanced approach

The DVF model is a balanced approach to design – meaning we must find the balance between:

- Customer appeal and interest
- Business strategy, risk appetite, financial constraints and budgets
- Capability to design and support.

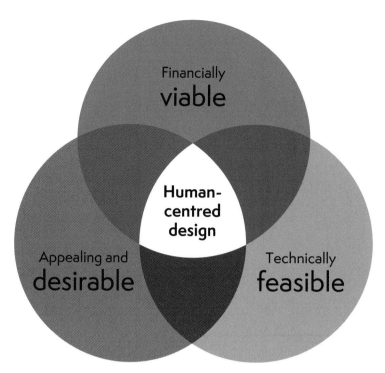

Figure 4 The DVF model

Adapted from IDEO U: https://www.ideou.com/blogs/inspiration/how-to-prototype-a-new-business

Desirability, viability, feasibility

The DVF model was created in the early 2000s by IDEO and was originally designed to help people build a new business (without going bankrupt). Since then, it's been used as a testing ground for all kinds of innovations, not just business design.

The DVF model asks you to test whether your business – or your solution, innovation or 'crazy new idea' – can positively answer three important questions:

- Is it appealing (desirability)?
- Can we achieve it (technical feasibility)?
- Can we afford it (financial viability)?

If you can't answer these three questions positively, your idea will almost certainly fail.

If your solution isn't desirable, nobody will want to use it.

If it isn't feasible, you won't find a way to design and support it.

If it isn't viable, you can't afford it.

As IDEO determined when it built the DVF model, the sweet spot for innovation is where viability, desirability and feasibility overlap in the Venn diagram shown in Figure 4. This is where your design efforts should focus: on a solution you can afford, that you're able to build, that your users will want.

This same sweet spot is the aim of human-centred design: it's a balance where the user achieves value from the service and the organisation receives value from the use of that service.

 **Over to you**

Can you see the value of adopting the DVF model in your IT service management?

What would be the biggest benefit of using the DVF model in your IT service management?

How to build a collaborative team in your IT service management with the DVF model

You can use the DVF model to make sure you have a collaborative team available for your design process in IT service management. You'll need people who can make sure the three DVF questions are answered with the right amount of insight and experience.

Firstly, you'll need someone who understands your users, so they can confirm (or deny!) that the solution you're considering is desirable to the people who will be using the service. Then you'll need someone with an understanding of your budget, so they can address questions about the financial viability. Finally, you'll need people who understand your IT department's capability, so they can work out whether the solution is technically feasible.

There are some other people who you might want to include:

- **For desirability** Include human-centred designers, product owners, market researchers and often frontline employees, as well as consumer advocates and community groups
- **For viability** Include representatives from the business, such as business product owners, organisational strategists, and financial and process experts
- **For feasibility** Include IT professionals, solution architects, support staff and procurement experts. This part of the model may also include industrial designers, architects, and experts outside the business such as governments and regulatory bodies.

Complete your collaborative team by including users

In Humanising IT, true collaboration encourages IT professionals to collaborate with users.

Collaboration encourages us to view users as active participants in the design of our solutions, getting them to take responsibility in order for value to be realised. The simple acts of interacting and engaging with users early in the design process can foster a sense of loyalty and even ownership. This relationship will make it easier for us to reach users later (if, let's say, we want to iterate our solutions in a cycle of 'continuous improvement'), and it may even encourage users to empathise with us.

This collaborative approach will also be beneficial if a solution doesn't meet all the requirements, or if there is a shortcoming that we didn't anticipate. (Of course, the best approach is not to make those mistakes in the first place, but few of us are perfect!)

When collaborating with users and colleagues, some useful questions include:

- Do they want it?
- Will it improve their life or work?
- Do we have the resources to launch it?
- Can we design and support it in an affordable way?
- Can we make (or save) money by delivering it?
- Is it aligned with our business outcomes and the organisation's mission?

 Key message

Human-centred design provides foundational concepts to consider when designing a new service, as well as evaluating current services (or the 'as is state').

The five Ps of human-centred design

We cover this concept in our next chapter, but we wanted to provide a brief overview. The five Ps of human-centred design are:

- People
- Place
- Products
- Partners
- Processes.

Asking questions that are aligned with the five Ps of human-centred design is also a great technique for creativity, brainstorming and collaboration.

An IT service management DVF checklist

When you next get the opportunity to collaborate with stakeholders to improve or create a new IT service, here's a handy checklist to make sure you've achieved full representation.

- Desirability:
    - Have you engaged users and customers?
    - Have you spoken with IT service desk analysts? Do you know how they like to work?
    - Have you included level 2 and 3 resolver groups? What kinds of communications and processes work well for them? Are you following the old model, or have you brainstormed a better way for service desk agents to engage with them?
    - What about suppliers and external partners – have you spoken to them?
    - Which processes and information work best for external partners? What doesn't work?

- Viability:
    - Have you explored other models of incident management in the event of the service failing or experiencing degradation?
    - Does the traditional IT service desk model work for the organisation? What other models could you brainstorm?
    - How could you leverage support staff in downtimes?
    - Is the current service management model sustainable?

- Feasibility:
    - What's the most feasible way to deliver your new service? (Fitting new processes and ways of working into existing systems may be the most feasible, but is it really going to achieve the right outcomes?)

Recap

In this chapter, we looked at one of the most fundamental strategies and tools that human-centred design employs: empathy. We provided great tips for empathy and looked at the limitations of using it.

We also explored the concept of personas, proto-personas and key user groups.

Then we examined some of the key tenets from human-centred design around creativity, brainstorming and collaboration. Perhaps the most refreshing concept we learned is that even we – IT professionals – can be creative!

We briefly studied the origins of human-centred design, and finally we explored the DVF model (desirability, viability and feasibility) and how you can make use of the model to build a human-centred design team that represents your users and IT professionals. We also included a checklist for DVF, and we highly encourage you to keep exploring the DVF model.

We hope you have enjoyed learning introductory concepts of human-centred design, and most importantly we hope you are starting to unearth the real potential of integrating human-centred design with IT service management – and that's exactly what we discuss in our next chapter. We look at the similarities (and differences) between traditional IT service management and human-centred design, and explore how we can and should integrate them to design great services that your users will love and that you will love designing and supporting.

Exciting stuff!

4 Integrating IT service management with human-centred design

 In this chapter, we will:

- Look at the similarities (and differences) between traditional IT service management and human-centred design
- See how we can unite both schools of thought around one shared concept: the experience of our customers, our users and our colleagues
- Examine the four Ps of IT service management and the five Ps of human-centred design, and how they can synchronise
- Take a high-level look at the Double Diamond model from human-centred design
- Encourage you to take a non-linear approach to IT service management.

The era of experience

We are in the era of experience, where customers are in the driving seat. Their expectations, desires and insights are leading to innovations in products and services.

This is as true in technology as it is in industries like health, finance and entertainment. Consider streaming cinema, teleconferencing and digital-only debit cards. Each of these is an innovation that was born from customer need, or is adapting to new and evolving customer expectations.

And yet, if you look at many of the IT departments that exist around the world, decades-old processes remain doggedly in place. An embedded approach based on a 'best practice is best' philosophy remains, in spite of rapid technological change.

The result is that the services IT departments deliver aren't necessarily connecting with what customers want, expect or need – at the time when customers want, expect and need them. Just to clarify, the services we're referring to don't mean the latest device or app – what we mean is the services from IT, like contacting the IT service desk, chasing up a service request or onboarding a new employee (I know what you're thinking: that should sit with people services. Unfortunately, IT seems to bear the brunt of poor user experience for this one.)

This means customers are missing out, and so are the IT professionals, who know they could be enjoying greater innovation and improvement, at a sustainable but still satisfying pace.

And do you know what customers and IT professionals have in common? They're humans. Same as you.

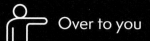

Over to you

In this section we have discussed how innovation was born from customer need, or is adapting to new and evolving customer expectations. Do you think Henry Ford would have the same sentiments when he said, 'If I had asked my customers what they wanted, they would have said a faster horse'?

Human-centred design and IT service management: Same same, but different?

So far, while we have been exploring human-centred design, we have also been providing snippets of how some tools and techniques could be used in IT service management. But how do you integrate a more in-depth human approach to IT service management? The good news: it isn't hard at all. Do you know why? Because they have some fundamental similarities and synergies.

You might be surprised how much they have in common. You might even have that lightbulb moment that I had, the one where I asked, 'How come we don't integrate human-centred design into IT service management?'

Meaning what we say, saying what we mean

Before we start exploring the integration of human-centred design into IT service management, let's start with some definitions:

- What do you call an IT service?
- How do you define IT service management?

If you're struggling to come up with answers, you're not alone. These terms are often misunderstood. Adding to the confusion, 'IT service management' is often used interchangeably with 'service management' – but do they really mean the same thing?

What does 'IT' mean?

In my research, I found no fewer than 20 definitions for 'IT service management'. We outlined some in Chapter 1. For simplicity and consistency, in this book we'll define the terms like this:

Definitions

- **IT service** A service provided by an IT department in order to support a business service.
- **IT service management** The management of the end-to end delivery of IT services to users.

So, an IT service supports a business service. But what is a business service?

Definition: Business service

A service that is delivered to business customers by users.

According to our definitions, then: successful delivery of business services can often depend on one or more IT services.

This brings us to another important distinction: customers and users. We defined these roles in Chapter 2, and, because of the importance of both definition and distinction in Humanising IT, we have outlined them again:

Definitions

- **Customer** The person deriving value from the business services.
- **User** The person using the technology to deliver value to the customer.

By our definition, a customer is the person the business serves. For an airline, it's the person travelling on the aircraft. For a hospital, it's the person arriving for their consultation.

The user, then, is the person who is using technology to deliver that service. It's the airline staff member who is using technology to determine the weight and balance of an aircraft prior to departure, or a check-in agent boarding passengers using a scanner provided by IT, or a flight controller using data analytics to determine the most optimal flying route.

At the hospital, the user is the nurse or doctor reading patient records from an application maintained by the IT department, which integrates with regulatory bodies. It could also be the receptionist or a staff member of the hospital's finance department; each is using technology to ultimately support business outcomes to achieve the organisation's mission.

Why is this distinction so important? To answer this question, let's hear from Chris Barrett, a transformational specialist, adviser and educator with a wealth of experience in redefining IT organisations across the globe. Through storytelling, Chris eloquently describes different roles within an organisation, and it's probably one of the best analogies to describe the role of IT service management that you will ever read. Who doesn't love a good story?

Now do we know what IT means?

Chris Barrett, transformation specialist, adviser and educator

Think of the business as the pilot of a major airline. The pilot's *customers* are the passengers on her plane.

The *users* are the people who perform business services. This includes the ground crew (such as baggage handlers, check-in agents and airport staff), engineering teams, air traffic control – and sometimes, even the co-pilot.

The pilot is dependent on the kit (the plane and its systems) to do her job and transport her passengers safely to their destination.

In this analogy, *IT service management* includes everyone involved in enabling the services used by the ground crew and pilot. They're the ones ensuring the kit is fit for purpose, uptime is (literally) maintained, the air space is clear, the pilot's instructions are being received, bags can be tracked – and so on.

The pilot knows how well the plane is flying and makes requests of the ground crew, and recommendations for a better flight.

Meanwhile, the ground crew monitors the flight and knows how the pilot is flying the plane, how to avoid turbulence, whether there are any fuel efficiencies to be gained, how often meals are being served, and whether the crew rosters are accurate. They make decisions based on information.

They communicate their experiences to IT, in the hopes of providing a safe, workable business service to the customers. Working together, the teams might identify things to fix (incidents), problems to solve (or workarounds to accept for known errors), upgrades to make (change requests) and even innovations to consider that could lead to transformations (for example, a change in aircraft).

In this analogy, where safety is a high priority, the business and IT are strongly motivated to work together. In a circumstance like this one, it's clear that an IT department can add value over and above a basic maintenance, break/fix mentality and service availability as typically outlined in service level agreements.

If the pilot and ground crew have a human interaction with a proactive IT department, then the relationship shifts from keeping the plane in the air to getting the most out of the experience for passengers, crew and other staff.

The IT department becomes a strategic partner.

Chris makes the point that the IT department and the business (the pilot) are strategic partners that work together to deliver value to the customers.

Over to you

How do you think your IT department is perceived in the wider business? Are you a trusted partner, or do you feel you've been left behind on the tarmac?

Is your IT service management stuck in 'break/fix' mode?

Do you feel like you're contributing to the customer experience, either directly or indirectly?

Can you see how you might be able to improve the customer experience from where you're seated?

That awkward family photo

Now that we have refined our definitions, let's explore the similarities between human-centred design and IT service management, with, of course, a little humour along the way.

IT service management and human-centred design have similar values and aspirations. Most obviously, they both aim to serve the customer.

To anyone outside the family, they seem to have a lot in common. Inside the family, though, they're more like cousins than siblings. They're related, sure, but they grew up apart and they don't really know each other all that well. And they've never learned how to communicate with each other. Until now.

The awkward family photo

Customer focus is something you do, not something you are

Key messages

- IT service management champions customer focus but doesn't tell us *how* to be customer focused
- Human-centred design shows us how to be customer focused, but falls short in understanding the complexity of designing and supporting the customer experience.

You know the difference between a noun and a verb, right? A verb is a doing word (run, act, laugh, achieve). A noun is a thing (hill, stage, table, school).

The thing about the word 'focus' is that it can be a noun or a verb. You can focus on something far away (like an achievement) and you can have a focus that is strong, clear, motivating – or the opposite. In short, the way you focus determines your focus.

What does this have to do with IT service management? Most IT professionals are smart, experienced and well intentioned. We may have studied and achieved certifications in several IT service management frameworks. These frameworks provide a solid foundation for managing technology services and serving our users.

So we should have all the tools we need to be customer focused. Right?

Think about it. If you wanted to improve your focus on your customers today, how would you do that?

Over to you

Have you ever been asked to 'be more customer focused'?

Was it clear what that meant – or *how* to be customer focused?

Do you know how you would measure the level of customer focus in your IT department?

We defined IT service management earlier. Let's share another definition of it that we found in our research. See if you can guess why we've included it here.

Another definition of IT service management

Service Management is a *customer-focused* approach to delivering information technology. Service Management focuses on providing value to the customer and also on the customer relationship. Service Management provides a framework to structure IT-related activities and the interactions of IT technical personnel with customers and clients.

UC Santa Cruz (italics ours)[39]

---

39   UC Santa Cruz. ITS service management: Key elements. https://its.ucsc.edu/itsm/servicemgmt.html.

Note that this definition includes a clear reference to customer focus. This is one of the few IT service management definitions that take the time to remind us that the customer is the reason we provide IT services in the first place.

Break then fix – is there anything else?

As Chris Barrett said in his analogy earlier in this chapter, IT service management has traditionally been designed based on a break/fix operating model. 'Break/fix' is an industry term that refers to:

> ... work involved in supporting a technology service when it fails in the normal course of its function and requires intervention by a support organization in order to be restored to working order
>
> Microsoft[40]

A break/fix operating model tracks technology performance (i.e. whether the tech is 'broken' or fixed), and is founded on metrics that we need to meet when working to fix the break. The metrics are usually formalised in service level agreements (SLAs).

This approach tends to put IT on the back foot, managing complaints about broken technology – or managing poorly designed and implemented IT services that are almost guaranteed to break. This leads directly to the kinds of perceptions of IT we outlined earlier: that it's complex, costly and slow. It also leads to IT service management design that's more concerned with stability, cost, standardisation and improvements than a proactive, innovative and customer-focused approach to design and support IT services.

In short, a break/fix operating model forces us to focus on fixing (or 'improving') broken technology. It's never about the experience of the person using or supporting the technology. In contrast, human-centred design aims to capture human needs, research the (human) problem and co-design solutions that respond to the human experience, in order to support the business outcomes and achieve the organisation's mission.

 Over to you

Is your IT department a break/fix organisation?

How much of your day is spent on improving a poor service versus working on technology transformations or improvement initiatives?

---

40 Microsoft. Support limitations for issues with Microsoft 365 Apps for enterprise or Microsoft 365 Apps for business. https://support.microsoft.com/en-us/office/support-limitations-for-issues-with-microsoft-365-apps-for-enterprise-or-microsoft-365-apps-for-business-0a02cd18-19be-4cfa-b430-3b53ea26920f.

There's more to service than service level agreements

The traditional IT service management design approach concentrates on meeting the service levels that have been agreed for technology performance. It's about providing a stable, cost-effective and standardised technology. To state the obvious: that's pretty important.

Here's something else that's important, which service level agreements have traditionally excluded: the perceptions and feelings users have for the IT services they're using, and the perceptions and feelings of the people supporting those services.

'Wait a minute ...' – you're probably thinking – 'But IT service desks ask users to complete a survey or provide some type of feedback.' Now we have a question for you: did you know our research shows the response rate for these types of surveys is lower than 5%? In Humanising IT, this is not our idea of gauging the user experience – more on that later.

Speaking of service level agreements and the human experience or the lack thereof, the following is a discussion by Chris Dolphin on the topic of 'human experience agreements' (which further publications in our Humanising IT series will be exploring in detail). Chris has extensive experience in IT service management and the airline industry (this is where I met Chris; in fact I had the opportunity to work with him in France). He is the former vice president of global customer care in one of the top ten travel technology companies in the world.

In the following discussion, Chris makes a very profound statement:

Customers do understand that IT can fail, and they will forgive you. What is much harder to forget or forgive is how you make them feel.

Remember that magic ingredient: *empathy*.

A discussion on human experience agreements

Chris Dolphin, CEO and founder of New Dimensions Consulting

Customer-centric companies are known to outperform their competitors simply because they have built a relationship and understanding of their customers' needs and how to anticipate their consistently changing requirements.

In the last 10 years, consumer needs have forced businesses to shift away from their traditional business models across most industries to focus on speed, experience and independence. Increasingly, we are seeing an acceleration of this change; however, while business evolved, some elements were slower to evolve with the new business model.

Let's take a look that some key areas which were slower to evolve:

- Service level agreements and key performance metrics
- Definition of the customer (end user)
- Identification and continuous evolution of the emotional needs of the customer, user and employees.

To remain relevant, companies will need to evolve these points from a leadership, cultural and technical standpoint across the organisation and their partner network by putting people (emotional element) at the core of what they do.

Most C-level executives understand the online/digital competitive space and how real-time undesirable situations such as a cyberattack, system unavailability or poor system stability can make or break companies and their positive brand perception. However, customers do understand that IT can fail, and they will forgive you. What is much harder to forget or forgive is how you make them feel.

This is why all levels within a company (including IT) must now take a fresh look at introducing human experience agreements to understand and retain customers through loyalty.

What's the difference between service level agreements and human experience agreements?

Service level agreements

Service level agreements are very important to businesses, and in most cases are needed to set minimum standards of expectation(s) between companies, partners and customers. However, there are distinct differences between traditional service level agreements and human experience agreements:

- Service level agreements are operational or project-related and linked to commercials/contracts, and in most situations do not evolve to meet the new business needs or measure the entirety of the IT services that comprise the business service
- Service levels do not measure the experience of customers, nor help determine the emotional satisfaction or loyalty of the customer
- Service levels often have penalties and rewards attached and, in some cases, may become a revenue stream based on underperformance or failure to deliver against the contracted service targets.

Human experience agreements

Human experience agreements are non-operational metrics and consider the customer's experience. These metrics help you to understand how satisfied or unsatisfied your customers are with their various interactions with your service:

- Human experience agreements involve obtaining feedback after each interaction with your service
- Human experience agreements are consumer-centric metrics that focus on the perceived value of a service; they are more concerned with outcomes (not outputs) and value standpoint
- These non-operational metrics provide your organisation with early warning indicators of how customers feel about using your products, and can provide tremendous insights on where your company needs to focus its improvement initiatives.

Do we still need traditional service level agreements?

There is still significant value in service level agreements and operational KPIs; however, it's important to shift our thinking. Service level agreements are typically linked to the availability or uptime of an IT service, whereas human experience agreements are linked to the usability of your service and, most importantly, the experience of your customers.

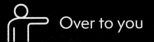
Giving credit where it's due: Service during a crisis

During the potentially catastrophic changes brought about by Covid-19, IT service management showed its strength. As the pandemic spread, most workforces mobilised quickly, pivoting to online services, teleconferencing, and implementing network security improvements and other measures that made working from home the new normal for millions of people around the world, all at once. A few years earlier, telehealth appointments, digital-only credit cards, and online delivery of classroom training and live theatre probably seemed radical.

IT departments managed to keep people working, expand network capacity, and repurpose software and apps to be more easily accessed online. An amazing and frankly heroic effort. And not a break/fix in sight.

So, how do we move from a regular break/fix operating model to a culture of empowerment, respect and recognition from colleagues and the business? How do we create a more positive experience, not just for users, but for our IT teams – and not just during a crisis?

The 'perfect integration' – it's time to start talking to each other

Let's get back to our estranged cousins: IT service management and human-centred design. Both have loyal and dedicated followers. Each group is confident that its way is the very best way to design and provide services.

They can't both be right, can they? After all, they seem so different. One is all about steadfastly following procedures, adhering to proven processes and striving to meet service levels. The other is far from cautious, rarely looks at processes, and enjoys challenging conventional ways of working. You could say one uses pessimism (break/fix) to keep things working and the other uses optimism (challenge, innovate) to identify new ways to work.

What if, by joining forces, each group can gain strength, experience and knowledge? It would take a brave leader to step outside traditional views to seek out the intersecting values and benefits in these groups. And it would take an innovative leader to identify the commonalities in order to unite and leverage the strengths of both groups.

It can be done. We've done it with Humanising IT! By boldly integrating IT service management into human-centred design (see Figure 5), we believe you can leverage the best from both worlds and create a better experience for your users. Which, in turn, can provide a better experience for your customers, your colleagues and you.

Figure 5 'The perfect integration': the intersection between IT service management and human-centred design

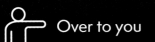 **Over to you**

Can you identify an IT service (or process) in your department that could benefit from more user focus?

Have you been part of designing a user-focused IT service management process? If so, what differences did it make for the user? What differences did it make for you and your IT colleagues?

Can we agree ... and disagree?

Back to that awkward family photo. Let's say our cousins are both car fanatics. On weekends, they retire to their individual garages, put on their overalls and tinker with vintage cars.

Great! So now we know they both like cars. But ... One cousin is all about vehicle safety. Her car has an advanced anti-lock braking system and a chassis so robust you could probably stop a tank with it. It's a safe ride, but it's not very comfortable.

Safe travelling versus comfortable travelling

The other cousin likes a smooth, comfortable experience when she's driving. She's put in extra suspension and plush upholstery over the car seat heaters. Comfy ride, but not very safe. For one thing, if you hit a pothole too hard, you could bounce right into the sun visor. Ouch!

Imagine if the cousins worked together to build one car that addressed all their priorities. They could combine their efforts to build a car that's both safe and comfortable, and warm and secure for all humans to experience.

After all, they're both working on cars. There has to be some common ground.

On the road safe – but maybe not so comfortable

Where IT service management and human-centred design are similar

Let's take a look at some of the similarities between our warring, car-loving cousins. We'll start with a very uncanny similarity (well, on first appearance). Both IT service management and human-centred design use a concept called the 'Ps'. IT service management has four Ps and human-centred design has five Ps – let's look at these seemingly similar concepts.

The four Ps of IT service management

IT service management uses four Ps to guide an organisation's IT service management strategy. The Ps play an integral role in how IT services are created. They are:

- **People** These need the right skills, the right knowledge, the right level of experience to be involved in the provision of IT services. Plus, their skills, knowledge and experience must be current and must align to business needs

- **Products** These are the technology management systems used to deliver IT services. When designing a new or changed service, IT service managers are expected to consider the capabilities these tools have, and how they'll enhance the delivery and support of agreed services

- **Partners** These include vendors, third-party software companies, manufacturers and other suppliers involved in the provision of IT services. Partners need to support IT service levels and business expectations

- **Processes** These are the 'how'. They are used to manage and support the services, in order to meet customer expectations and agreed service levels. All processes must be measurable.

Let's take a closer look at the first – and arguably the most important – P of the four Ps of IT service management: people.

Which people? Customers or users or...?

The four Ps concept describes people in terms of their skills, knowledge and experience. It doesn't describe people as, well, people. It doesn't look at the humanity of people, or their human-ness.

It also, crucially, leaves out several groups of people. It describes people – IT people – as *resources*. There are no people-as-users or people-as-customers. Let's see what human-centred design does with its Ps.

The five Ps of human-centred design

Human-centred design provides foundational concepts to consider when designing a new service, as well as when evaluating current services (or the 'as is state').

The five Ps of human-centred design (see Figure 6) are:

- **People** These are the 'who' behind design efforts. It emphasises empathy with the human experience at all levels of design.
- **Place** Human-centred design asks where the services and products will be created, delivered and experienced (by the people, above).
- **Products** These are the tangible objects and collateral used to inform or deliver the service. Human-centred design considers how products will be used by the humans in the field, and is open to making adjustments to the products accordingly.
- **Partners** These include the external providers that help to produce or enhance the service or product. These may be vendors, trainers or other professionals that we rely on to connect their expertise with the needs of the people we're designing for, in a timely way.
- **Processes** These include the workflows, routines and workarounds that enable us to get the job done. Human-centred design looks at the way things are done from the human experience of the user.

 Key messages

- You may have noticed that the five Ps describe elements of the design process that are significant to the human experience of all the humans involved. Not just the users, but also the IT professionals and the third-party vendors – and everyone else.
- The five Ps of human-centred design correspond almost directly with the classic five questions for any solution: who, where, what, when and how.

But wait! There's more.

People	Place	Products	Partners	Processes
It's about everyone's experience; your team is as responsible as you are	Physical and digital environments where services are created, delivered and experienced	These are the tangible objects and collateral used to inform or deliver the service	Any external providers that help to produce or enhance the service	To understand the workflows, routines and workarounds to 'get the job done'

Figure 6 The five Ps of human-centred design

There are two more Ps in human-centred design

The five Ps comprise the standard human-centred design approach. Recently, though, there's been a trend to adopt two more Ps – *planet* and *purpose*. (Seems like human-centred design loves a P.)

- **Planet** This P challenges designers to consider the environmental and long-term effects of production and design decisions. It ensures that we consider the materials and resources we plan to use, and the impact this will have on the natural environment and people's behaviour. It also identifies the legacy of the product or service.

  Interestingly, this sixth P borrows from and adapts a concept known as the *triple bottom line*.

 Definition: The triple bottom line

'The triple bottom line is a business concept that posits firms should commit to measuring their social and environmental impact – in addition to their financial performance – rather than solely focusing on generating profit, or the standard "bottom line". It can be broken down into "three Ps": profit, people, and the planet.'[41]

Wait a minute … did you notice another P in the triple bottom line concept: profit? (Like we said, P is popular.)

- **Purpose** The goal of the seventh P is to challenge the organisation to consider its social and ethical responsibilities. It asks what social impact the organisation wants to create. Increasingly, we can witness organisations considering their impact beyond profits and losses. Like the planet P, this P identifies the legacy that organisations hope to leave.

Now let's take a look at some other similar concepts from IT service management and human-centred design.

---

41   Harvard Business School. The triple bottom line: What it is & why it's important.
     https://online.hbs.edu/blog/post/what-is-the-triple-bottom-line.

Value chains and the Double Diamond

At its core, a value chain is a sequence of activities to deliver value. In the context of IT service management, this might include anything from software development to service delivery and support. By understanding the value chain, IT departments can identify inefficiencies and improvements, which can lead to better outcomes for both the organisation and its customers.

Meanwhile, in human-centred design, the *Double Diamond model*[42] is used to represent the creative process of designing a product or service, from problem through to solution. The Double Diamond breaks the creative process down into:

- Finding out what problems need to be solved
- Designing the solutions that will be used.

Note that both the Double Diamond and the service value chain aim to deliver products and services. They even look alike!

The Double Diamond model: An overview

We'll explore the Double Diamond in more detail in Chapter 5. For now, let's have a quick introduction so we can compare it with a simple service value chain (see Figures 7 and 8).

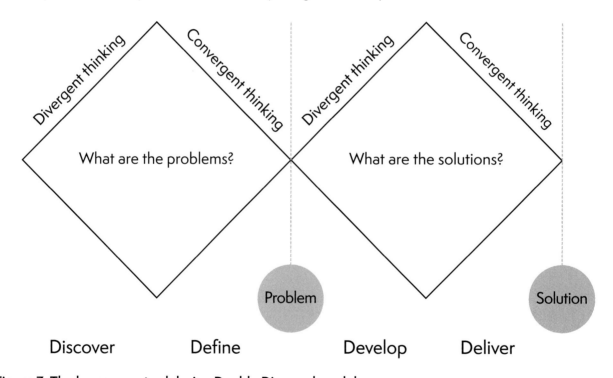

Figure 7 The human-centred design Double Diamond model

Double Diamond model used courtesy of the Design Council (https://www.designcouncil.org.uk/)

---

42   Use of the Double Diamond model is provided courtesy of the Design Council. https://www.designcouncil.org.uk/.

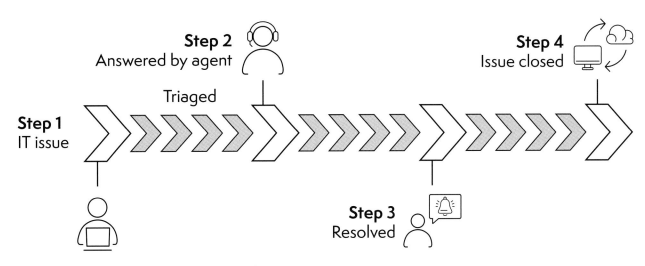

Figure 8 An example of a simple value chain

The Double Diamond model in Figure 7 is a graphical representation of the design and innovation process that is at the heart of human-centred design. It shows how to take a structured approach to challenging problems and designing solutions, based on a thorough understanding of customer needs.

> The Double Diamond is the simplest shape to connect ideas, codifying experiences by tapping into our emotions and redefining our physical world.
>
> Ed Gardiner[43]

The first diamond takes steps to reach a clear problem definition. The second diamond moves from problem definition to solution.

Phases of the first diamond (diamond 1)

The first diamond focuses on arriving at a clear definition of the problem – without assumptions. It includes two phases:

- **Discover** Speaking to and spending time with people who are affected by the problem
- **Define** Using the insights collected from the discover phase to define the challenge in a different way. Sometimes this results in the identification of a different problem to what was initially assumed, or to a complete *reframing* of the problem.

Reframing

Reframing is another technique used in human-centred design and I highly encourage you to adopt it in IT service management. As defined below, reframing encourages you to be innovative and think about future opportunities for a problem – this technique could (and should) be used for re-designing how we design and support IT services.

---

43   Ed Gardiner, Behavioural design lead at Warwick Business School. Quoted in 'Reframing the problem' by Manish Chauhan (2020). https://medium.com/the-experience-of-design/reframing-the-problem-b85a87d3747a.

Definition: Reframing

'Reframing is a design thinking skill as well as a strategic skill. Reframing enables designers to come up with fresh and compelling solutions that act upon a future world. Reframing enables strategists to map possible directions through strategic frameworks and identify future business opportunities.'[44]

Example of reframing: A packaged dilemma for Fly First Airlines

Let's visit our friends at Fly First Airlines to see how the reframing technique is used on an issue concerning the airline's major service offering.

A primary revenue stream for Fly First is offering packaged holiday deals to both existing and potential customers. These packaged holiday deals include flights, hotels and car hire.

With low-cost competitors entering the market, the airline is experiencing a significant decrease in sales of their once highly popular packaged holiday deals. Shalini (the service owner of packaged holidays) knows that competing on price is possible, but with an already saturated market she is unsure of what options she could use to increase sales.

As a forward thinker, Shalini engages Tobiah, a human-centred designer. With sales decreasing day by day, she wants to ensure that both her assumptions and solutions are correct.

The problem statement from the business point of view is:

'We are losing revenue to an increasingly competitive and price-driven market on our packaged holiday deals. To compete, we need to lower our prices and aggressively pursue more sales.'

Before proposing any solutions, Tobiah conducts research, interviewing a diverse range of customers. The research identifies three important themes:

- Packaged holiday deals offered by most airlines are similar and are often to the same destinations
- Customers who had previously travelled on a packaged holiday are unlikely to book the same holiday again – they want new and exciting destinations (i.e. they are bored with the limited choices offered by airlines)
- Customers who had not travelled on a packaged deal perceive these types of holidays as boring.

Tobiah reframes the problem statement as:

'After years of offering the same package holiday deals, our existing customers are bored – and with little product differentiation, there is no real incentive for new customers to choose Fly First Airlines over any other airline.'

By reframing the problem from the customer's point of view, Shalini and her team can see that market differentiation is part of the problem – it isn't only about price. Working with Shalini and her team, Tobiah is able to start designing the right solution which includes new package deals, focusing on unique and exciting destinations, appealing to both budget- and not-so-budget-conscious holiday makers.

---

44   Reframing Studio. Reframing method. https://www.reframingstudio.com/reframing-method.

It doesn't matter how great your solution is if you're working on the wrong problem. It's essential to take the time to understand what you're solving.

There are many ways to reframe, and each project requires a different approach – it's important to work with someone who has experience. Often, as designers reframe, they look to the impact on people and what they're trying to achieve – this ensures that the intended customer outcomes are front and centre.

'How might we'

A further technique used as part of reframing is termed 'how might we'.

After gaining a holistic view of the problem, the other typical way that designers reframe the problem is to turn it into a *how-might-we* question. In these cases, we turn the issues into a springboard for ideas and better solutions. Conversely, designers use the how-might-we format because it suggests that a solution is possible and because the question offers us the chance to answer it in a variety of ways.

The list below provides some excellent techniques and examples of how-might-we questions for an airport-centric experience:[45]

- **Amp up the good** How might we use the kids' energy to entertain fellow passengers?
- **Remove the bad** How might we separate the kids from fellow passengers?
- **Explore the opposite** How might we make the wait the most exciting part of the trip?
- **Question an assumption** How might we entirely remove the wait time at the airport?
- **Go after adjectives** How might we make the rush refreshing instead of harrowing?

A well-framed how-might-we does not include a solution; rather it provides a great *frame* for innovative thinking.

 Over to you

Can you identify a problem that you would reframe within IT service management?

How might the solution look different to the way it is used today?

If I were given one hour to save the planet, I would spend 59 minutes defining the problem and one minute resolving it.

Albert Einstein[46]

---

45   Kimberly Crawford (2018). Design thinking toolkit, activity 16 – How might we ...?
      https://spin.atomicobject.com/2018/12/12/how-might-we-design-thinking/

46   Albert Einstein is quoted as saying this, but there is no definite proof.

The incident management process is broken – is it?

Katrina Macdermid

An example of reframing and how-might-we in IT service management

A recent engagement by a major Australian company provides a great example of how I have used reframing and the *how-might-we* technique within IT service management.

My client was in a spot of bother (to say the least). The company provides IT service management expertise to over 30 clients both nationally and internationally. Its largest client was threatening to cancel its contract – incident volumes were increasing and incidents were taking too long to close.

My remit: improve the incident management process. It seemed to make sense: if we improved the process, incidents would decrease and tickets could be closed sooner. Right? Hmmm …

Of course, during my engagement, I employed human-centred design techniques: following the define process within the first diamond, we *reframed* the problem.

It turned out that the incident management process was probably the most robust process the company had. The real problem was that tickets were being logged incorrectly. In our discover phase, we found that over 40% of tickets logged were actually the result of user error, or lack of knowledge of how to use IT services or applications.

Following a series of workshops using the how-might-we technique (using lots of Post-it notes), we were able to reframe the problem. Some of our Post-it notes read:

- *How might we* educate and empower our users to better use our IT services?
- *How might we* design our services so that they are more intuitive and easier to use?
- *How might we* better design the incident logging process so users could resolve their issues?

My client now had the right problem to solve, and began activities such as:

- Immediate investment in knowledge management
- Working with the right teams to ensure user experience formed part of the design of IT services and applications
- Improving the ticket-logging tooling and process.

And now the incident management process was able to do just that: manage (real) incidents!

Phases of the second diamond (diamond 2)

The second diamond includes the phases where the solution is developed and delivered. Remember that by the time we reach this diamond, the problem has been clearly defined.

- **Develop** Developing, iterating and evaluating potential solutions until a shortlist of clear winners emerges
- **Deliver** Testing different solutions at small scale, rejecting those that won't work and improving the ones that will.

The develop and deliver phases shown in Figure 9 encourage us to give different answers to the problem, to seek inspiration from elsewhere, and to co-design a solution with a range of people.

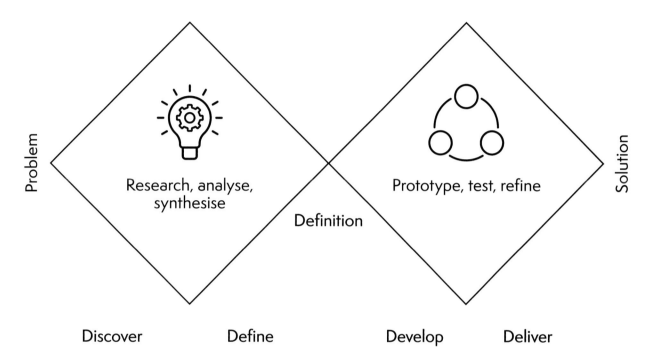

Figure 9 Human-centred design Double Diamond model

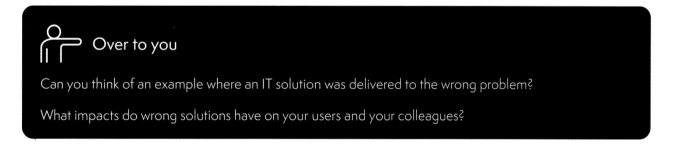

Over to you

Can you think of an example where an IT solution was delivered to the wrong problem?

What impacts do wrong solutions have on your users and your colleagues?

All right – that's it for our very quick overview of the human-centred design Double Diamond model. Let's take a look at IT value chains.

IT value chains: An overview

The concept of value chains (see Figure 8) as used in some IT service management frameworks is in many ways very similar to the Double Diamond – but this time it might not seem so obvious. Why? Because when we design IT products and services, we are not typically encouraged to be creative (like we are in the Double Diamond) – we usually have constraints such as timelines, budgets and resource availability holding us back, along with the preconceived idea that best practice is best. So, although IT value chains are a graphical representation of the activities needed to create a product or service, there isn't a great deal of encouragement or many techniques provided to deviate from the 'best practice' path.

When designing a product or service, we loosely follow these phases:

- **Plan** Detailing and communicating steps required to achieve the outcome
- **Build** Buying or creating the technical components
- **Run** Operationalising the service and ongoing support.

 Key message

In my view, perhaps the main reason for the lack of design for the human experience within IT service management is the approach to designing services. Did you notice in the above definitions of each phase that there was no mention of the experience of customers, users or IT professionals?

Again, this was just a very quick overview – remember that this book is not about in-depth learning of concepts. Now let's see how these two approaches can synergise and synchronise.

Taking a closer look at the family connection

When we start to map the Ps of IT service management to the phases of a typical IT value chain and human-centred design, we can begin to see how closely related our estranged cousins are, as Table 2 shows.

Table 2 Mapping the components of IT service management, IT value chains and human-centred design

IT value chain phases	Human-centred design Double Diamond phases	The Ps of IT service management and human-centred design
Plan	Discover	People
Plan	Define	People, partners
Build	Develop	Products
Build	Define, develop	Partners, processes
Run	Deliver	Processes, place

Pretty close connection, right? It also gives us an idea of why we get into so many difficulties with vocabulary between business teams, IT teams, digital teams and well, lots of other teams. What is important is that each approach has a valuable contribution to make to our understanding of the problem and how to address the problem. The difficulty lies in the way people have become siloed into a particular way of working.

What we're doing in this book is opening doors between the groups and allowing people to understand, adopt and adapt concepts from approaches in order to design and support IT services.

 **Over to you**

Can you identify where some of these activities or phases could integrate when you design IT services?

It's not that straight

In the previous section, we laid out the key concepts of the Double Diamond model and the IT value chains.

But don't be deceived! Just because we can list them linearly, this doesn't mean the processes themselves are anywhere near linear. In fact, both approaches are decidedly non-linear in the delivery and support of products and services:

- **IT value chains: the non-linear approach to delivering value** The phases in value chains represent steps to deliver value to customers. Keep in mind, though, that a service may have different orders and combinations. Not all steps will be required for every service

- **Double diamond: the non-linear approach to understanding the problem and how to solve it** Human-centred designers are encouraged to move back and forth between the phases of the Double Diamond in order to fully understand what the problem is and how they can either solve it, or improve on an existing solution.[47]

This means that you're free to dip into each activity (or phase) as you need it. You can revisit phases (or activities) throughout the design-and-deliver process, and you can use some of the tools from the beginning of your project to assess how the project outcomes have resulted with the humans making use of them.

For creative people, that's great news! It means you don't have to feel stuck in a rigid and siloed way of working. For people who don't see themselves as creative (yet), that news can be daunting.

Don't panic. Just play. We encourage you to make use of each activity or phase as and when you need it. Try it out. See how it fits and whether it works for you, your teams and your users. Don't be afraid to try something else if you still need more clarity or fresh ideas.

---

47   Justinmind. The Double Diamond model: What is it and should you use it?
      https://www.justinmind.com/blog/double-diamond-model-what-is-should-you-use/.

> ### ⚙ Key message
>
> There are activities that you will need to do in the right order, which you can follow in detail or loosely. For example, you should never jump into ideation without research – you can't develop solutions if you don't know the 'why' or have insights on hand. Meaning, if you don't validate, challenge or research your current understanding, then you won't know if you are designing the right thing.
>
> Not following certain design paths can be a potentially costly and dangerous exercise, resulting in a poor experience – which, after all, defeats the purpose of human-centred design.

Feel free to ask others for their insights and ideas. This might be people in other teams, or people from your partner organisations. It might also be your users and their customers. When it comes to solving problems to design and support IT services, you should never feel alone.

A happy family connection

Recap

In this chapter, we've taken a high-level overview of some of the most popular concepts in IT service management and human-centred design, and shown how they can (and should) integrate harmoniously. Hopefully you've been able to see how they can be united around a common focus (customer focus, user focus and IT professional focus!), and you've been inspired to start thinking about how to use the Ps of IT service management with the Ps of human-centred design. We hope you've found insights from exploring the phases of the IT value chains and those of the Double Diamond model (or both!) to invigorate your own approach to design and support IT services.

In Chapter 5, we'll talk tactics: ways of thinking, ways of researching and ways of testing. We'll drill deeper into the Double Diamond model. We'll also examine the design process from end to end, focusing on the phases at the beginning of the Double Diamond: defining the problem (ensuring we are fixing the right problem).

The techniques we are learning can (and should) be used to improve the user experience (and yours), and build relationships with users and their customers to support business outcomes and to meet your organisation's mission.

5 Drilling into the Double Diamond

 In this chapter, we will:

- Take another look at the Double Diamond model and some of the tactical tools that can make the design journey easier
- Look at divergent and convergent thinking during the design process
- Talk about the two main approaches to research: quantitative and qualitative
- Take a detour into a trap of research (and some tips for dealing with it)
- Take a deeper dive into the first diamond of the Double Diamond model, which will help you define the problem you're designing for
- Learn more about the non-linear approach to the design process
- Hear from Sami Kallio, CEO of Happy Signals, on how experience management will drive better business operations and outcomes
- Hear an intriguing story from Professor Michael Buist about how he used technology to change a somewhat dogmatic and unfavourable culture within the healthcare industry
- Hear from Barry Anderson, a change advocator and transformational specialist.

Getting back into the diamonds

Let's return to the Double Diamond model from human-centred design: see Figure 9.

As you probably remember, the Double Diamond represents the creative process of designing a product or service. The first diamond is dedicated to defining which problems need to be solved. The second is all about discovering which solutions will be delivered.

Diamond 1 takes us from problem to definition, and diamond 2 moves from definition to solution. Here's another way to think about it:

- Diamond 1 is where you make sure you're 'designing the right thing'
- Diamond 2 helps ensure you're 'designing the thing *right*'.

Stick with us as we drill a little further into the phases of the diamonds.

Human-centred design is a specialised skill

Experts in this field work for years honing their skills and their craft. We can only give you a snippet of these tools and concepts at a high level, but we encourage you to keep practising and learning.

Diamond phases

To state the obvious, the Double Diamond model consists of two diamonds, and each diamond has two phases (shown in detail in Figure 10).

Diamond 1: Designing the right thing

The first diamond includes the initial phases where the problem is defined. To do that, you carefully and thoroughly research the problem in order to build your understanding. Then, and only then, are you ready to articulate the problem (or problems) in specific terms. The two phases for the first diamond are:

- **Discover** Gain insights into the problem
- **Define** Determine and articulate the problem you'll focus on.

Diamond 2: Designing the thing right

The second diamond includes the phases where potential solutions are developed, tested and finally delivered:

- **Develop** Build or prototype some potential solutions
- **Deliver** Ensure the working solutions are released to the users.

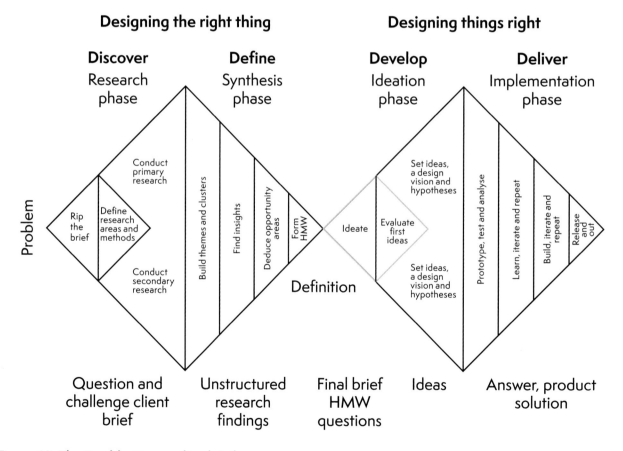

Figure 10 The Double Diamond in detail

Take a look at the figure of the two diamonds in Figure 10. Notice how the first phase of each diamond – research or ideation – moves from the narrow point on the left of the diamond and expands out to the widest point in the middle. Then, in the second phase – synthesis or implementation – the diamond narrows in again. In this way, the diamonds represent two critical ways of thinking; this concept is explained below.

Human-centred design for IT service management

How to think: divergent and convergent

We briefly discussed the concept of divergent and convergent thinking in Chapter 3. In this chapter we explore these types of thinking in greater detail, because they're a key component of Humanising IT.

You've probably already used divergent and convergent thinking without even knowing it.

Divergent thinking is the process of exploring and expanding. It's creative. It opens up and questions everything. Divergent thinking is about casting a wide net and gathering as many details and ideas as you can. There's no time for assumptions in divergent thinking. It's all about expanding the field.

Convergent thinking, on the other hand, is analytical. It's about assessing, refining, eliminating and prioritising solutions and ideas. Convergent thinking aims to select or narrow the possibilities identified during the divergent thinking phases.

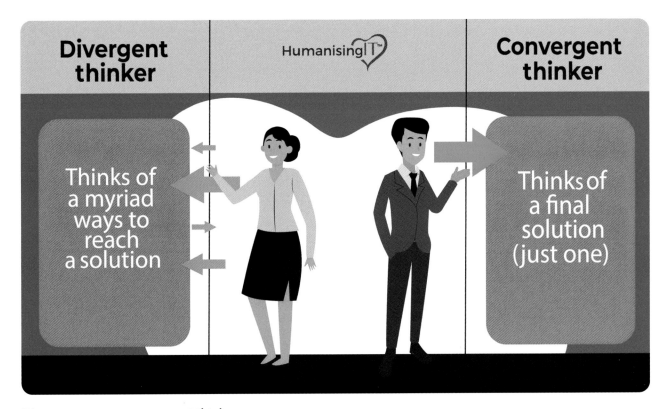

Divergent versus convergent thinkers

Both these ways of thinking are valuable parts of the process of designing a solution – so long as they're used at the right time. In essence, when you employ divergent thinking, you're thinking widely and creatively. When you use convergent thinking, you're being analytical and taking deep, focused action. Both these types of thinking are used in the Double Diamond approach (see Figure 11).

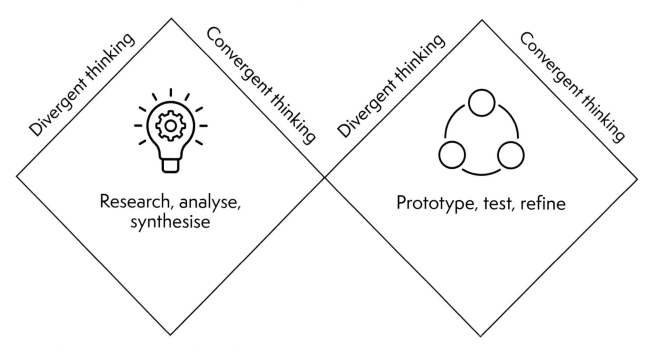

Figure 11 The Double Diamond model – divergent versus convergent thinking illustrated

 Definitions

- **Divergent thinking** 'Divergent thinking, also referred to as lateral thinking, is the process of creating multiple, unique ideas or solutions related to a problem that you are trying to solve. Divergent thinking is similar to brainstorming in that it involves coming up with many different ideas to solve a single problem.'[48]

- **Convergent thinking** 'Convergent thinking occurs when the solution to a problem can be deduced by applying established rules and logical reasoning. This type of reasoning involves solving a problem within the context of known information and narrowing down the solution based on logical inference.'[49]

If you keep this approach in mind, of expanding your list of possibilities and then narrowing in on inevitabilities, you'll start to see how human-centred design is used to develop creative solutions that *work*.

Which thinker are you?

Human-centred design encourages us to use both divergent and convergent thinking, so long as we're using them at the appropriate part of the design process.

Generally, divergent thinkers are able to generate many ideas and possibilities. They're open to talking to users and exploring elements that reveal themselves only in the process of research. When it comes to delivering solutions, a divergent thinker is someone who's able to envision how something might work in multiple ways. They're the sort of person you want on your team to help you 'think outside the box'.

---

48   Study.com. Divergent thinking: Definition & examples (video and lesson transcript).
      https://study.com/academy/lesson/divergent-thinking-definition-examples-quiz.html.

49   William D. S. Killgore (2010). Effects of sleep deprivation on cognition. In *Progress in Brain Research*.
      https://www.sciencedirect.com/topics/psychology/convergent-thinking.

Convergent thinkers, meanwhile, are able to assess ideas and solutions. They can separate elements and maintain a view of the big picture. They can quickly understand which information is relevant and which isn't. In the process of working through options, they're able to cost and scope suggestions rapidly, dismissing unaffordable options that offer little to no return on investment – and they can refine and add value to the ideas that will provide affordable solutions.

You may find, though, that you're more naturally inclined towards one form of thinking over the other. Don't let that stop you from trying both. You might surprise yourself with how much you can achieve. Many divergent thinkers become excellent convergent thinkers when called upon to fill that role, and vice versa.

 Key message

In Humanising IT, we discourage an IT service management culture of 'we've tried it before' or 'that won't work because …'

Sometimes you'll need to think creatively and be open-minded. You'll need to embrace risks and failure, and stay optimistic during phases that might feel fraught with complexity and detail. That takes divergent thinking. At other times, you'll be called on to think analytically, assess data, dismiss options, and call out when you identify issues. That's convergent thinking.

A word of warning: never attempt to use both divergent thinking and convergent thinking at the same time. Keep the divergent and convergent activities separate, so you're able to get into (and stay in) the right mindset for the phase of work you're in.

 Key message

Divergent and convergent mindsets require a different 'vibe' – and often different people are involved:

- **Divergent thinking** Engage in fun activities with your team and involve naturally curious people. Play games that make people laugh or ask everyone to participate in some creative drawing or entertaining activity.
- **Convergent thinking** Ask people that are problem solvers and like to be challenged. This time play a game based on calculation (not luck). Set a goal for your team where they need to problem-solve together or complete a logical task.

 Over to you

Do you consider yourself to be more of a divergent than a convergent thinker?

How might this technique better allow IT professionals to design and support IT services?

Why improvement in IT service management needs experience management

Sami Kallio, CEO of Happy Signals

The increased corporate reliance on IT drives higher employee expectations, so it's essential to understand where the reliance is and what it looks like. Some of this insight will potentially come from traditional IT service management feedback mechanisms such as customer satisfaction (CSAT) questionnaires and periodic service-level reviews. However, these traditional mechanisms only provide hints and clues about the employee's experience, being more transactional in nature and focused solely on service level metrics. Experience management goes beyond transactions to give better insight into how well different aspects of IT service delivery and support are performing – not in operational efficiency and effectiveness terms, but in relation to the outcomes experienced and expected by employees.

When asked what end-users want, a sensible IT response could be, 'To meet the agreed service levels'. It's a valid answer but not necessarily the best one. Instead, an employee might answer, 'To work flexibly from anywhere' or 'To respond quickly to customers'. There's currently a difference between what an IT service provider considers most important (and will measure), and what an employee will deem to be so. Plus, the measurements tend to be taken at the point of service creation, not service consumption. Service level agreements were never designed to measure experience, so it's no surprise that they don't. This means that there's an operational focus at the expense of delivered outcomes.

Without experience data, an IT service provider is blind to many employee issues and will make decisions based on misinformation and gut feelings. This could include the introduction of new technology-based capabilities designed to improve experiences that, in fact, do the opposite – with IT self-service portals providing a great example.

The complexity of technology and the constant need for change are permanent things in IT. They will always influence employee experience. But how do you know whether the increased complexity of the infrastructure better meets the business's needs? There might be improvements in scalability, availability, changeability and cost saving, but do they make an employee's work life easier, make business operations run better, and achieve superior outcomes? The problem is that the IT service provider doesn't know – because there's minimal insight into whether the increased complexity in infrastructure is helping or hindering people in their work, and business operations as a consequence. This issue becomes apparent when surveying sentiment and using experience-related measurements.

AI-enabled IT service management capabilities can help improve service delivery and support across all three of the IT service demands to be 'better, faster and cheaper'. However, organisational change management (OCM) tools and techniques are needed to address the people-change elements of AI introduction. There are also vital roles for experience data. First, in identifying the priorities for AI use (e.g. where is the greatest need for AI enablement, and where will it deliver the most significant benefits?), and second, in ensuring that the new AI-enabled capabilities actually deliver better operations and outcomes for people.

Experience data allows an IT service provider to focus its changes and improvements on 'what matters most' and ensure that improvement initiatives deliver as expected. Without it, an organisation will likely forge on with the best intentions but lack the insight needed to maximise the business value of its improvement investments. This means that:

- Employees will continue to lose time and productivity
- The IT service provider will continue to spend money in areas that don't create business value
- Good employees will be lost because of poor IT experiences.

Importantly, experience data and insight offer more than just the opportunity to make minor improvements in IT service management. While an IT service provider might start with, for example, small service desk changes, they can then progress to making more significant budgeting decisions based on the experience data. This is the future of experience management – using experience data for IT service management and broader IT decision-making to drive better business operations and outcomes.

 Key message

Divergent thinking is a way to articulate and identify ideas for how we can better design IT service management. Convergent thinking can ascertain which ideas will be the most cost-effective (providing the most value for the cost).

How to research: quantitative and qualitative

If you've done any kind of research before, you're probably already familiar with the differences between quantitative and qualitative research methods:

- **Quantitative research** As the label implies, this is all about numbers. Quantitative research describes *what* happens rather than *why* it happens, so it's a yes/no or 'How strongly do you agree?' type of research approach. Using quantitative research, you can create and analyse databases and quantities, which means numbers and percentages

- **Qualitative research** This is about collecting, analysing and interpreting non-numerical data. It focuses on people's experiences and interactions rather than data. A qualitative research method we've mentioned already in this book is observation (remember the squishy toothbrush?). Qualitative research also includes open-ended questions in a survey or interview. It's more than yes/no or choosing a number out of ten. It's about people describing a particular process, situation or experience from their point of view.

Let's explore both those methods of research in more detail, as they are great techniques that Humanising IT strongly encourages all IT service management professionals to adopt.

Quantitative research is about the numbers

Quantitative research is mostly used when there are databases of information. This type of research describes *what* happens rather than why it happens, and is common for economic and mathematical topics. It doesn't care about the motives that people have.

Usually, this type of research is helpful for describing what's happening with an existing circumstance, product or service. It may be market research or a survey. Numbers can tell you whether a product is selling or not.

The quantitative approach allows you to reach a higher sample size and collect information quickly. When you can study a larger sample size for any hypothesis, it's easier to reach an accurate generalised conclusion.

An example of quantitative research is analysis of website usage. You can tell how often your page is used, for how long and at what time of day. However, quantitative analysis alone won't tell you *why* people use the website when they do, and it won't tell you much about *who* those people are. Another disadvantage is that you won't necessarily know which metrics to set up in order to measure behaviour. For these reasons, quantitative research should be supported by qualitative analysis.

Qualitative research is basically about everything else

Qualitative research can involve various activities. Conducting and analysing interviews, recording videos, and observing people in their specific situations are the most common approaches and afford researchers a deeper understanding of the 'why'. While conducting the research, the users and frontline staff, their interactions, motivations and behaviour, are the focus.

One-on-one consultations and focus groups are a regular component of qualitative research. Remember to consider age, gender, ethnicity, social status, occupation, location and any other factors that might influence your research. Most importantly, you should engage with the people who are experiencing the problem that you're aiming to solve.

Qualitative interview technique

A qualitative interview is a conversation. The human-centred design practitioner seeks to understand the other person's ideas, beliefs, motives, choices and preferences in order to design a potential solution to the specific problem the user is having.

The designer or researcher directs and guides the interview in a structured but open way.

A research trap and some tips

Research is a vital part of the design process. You'll need your research skills the whole way through: not just when you're defining the problem, but also when you start to deliver prototypes and iterations later. But (isn't there nearly always a but?) here is a trap that can lead research – and researchers – astray.

Confirm whether you have confirmation bias

If you conduct research in order to prove a point or validate a position or a thought you already had, then watch out – you have a bad case of confirmation bias!

Confirmation bias is the tendency to interpret information in a way that supports our existing biases. It's the opposite of divergent thinking, and it's not convergent thinking, either. It's about being closed-minded and refusing to see anything that might contradict your assumptions.

Definition: Confirmation bias

'The tendency to interpret new evidence as confirmation of one's existing beliefs or theories.'[50]

You've probably already seen surveys that include confirmation bias. They ask questions like:

- What do you like about working on the IT service desk?
- How much has our new app improved your life?
- What's the best thing about us?

Know how (and when) to ask for feedback from users

Human-centred design advocates the importance of feedback – and to a large extent, so do most IT service management frameworks. However, let's look at the relatively narrow approach typically used to obtain feedback in IT service management.

An IT service desk typically asks for users' feedback at the end of an interaction. But by then, users might be so glad, relieved or grateful that they're not necessarily honest about the experience they've had. They also might forget some critical details in the process (that occurred during the interaction – not at the end) that we could use to avoid issues in the future or improve our IT service management.

Human-centred design encourages us to empathise with users at each touchpoint of a process, not just at the end. An IT service desk survey with a human-centred design approach might aim to identify:

- How users feel when they receive an automated update to their request
- How they feel when they *don't* receive an automated update
- How they feel when a ticket is given the status of 'closed, known error'.

Until we know the answers to questions like these – and others – how can we possibly design an IT support service that offers the best possible human experience for our users (and IT support staff)?

Understand the difference between data and insights

Data consists of the raw and unprocessed facts that we capture according to agreed-upon standards. The number of logins on our site, the number of downloads of our annual report and the time of year when most of those downloads happen. The number of calls or email requests received by our IT service desk. These are all examples of data.

Insights are the result of applying our knowledge and experience to the data. They are obtained through analysis and thought. We know, for example, that the volume of IT service desk calls declines in December – but until we conduct an analysis, we can't say for sure why the change occurs (though we can guess!). Insights are gained 'by analysing data and information in order to understand the context of a particular situation and draw conclusions. Those conclusions lead to actions you can apply to your business.'[51]

---

50   Lexico. https://www.lexico.com/definition/confirmation_bias.

51   Voccii. Data vs information vs insight. https://voccii.com/data-information-insight.

An insight tells you why something is happening. It reveals the deeper, unseen and less obvious forces at work that can be revealed only through an in-depth understanding. It unveils a new way of thinking that forces us to re-examine things, and shows us what is driving behaviour and patterns in such a way that we have a fresh perspective on the things in front of us.

Insights illuminate, expand our minds, help us to understand, and inspire us to do great things. They make sense of the world in a way that we can action. Once we know to anticipate changes to call volumes, we can adjust our resourcing accordingly.

 Key message

Turning data and research into insights is a critical skill that many people – through practice and experience – can excel at.

We encourage you to develop your skills in creating (and testing) your insights. Keep practising!

What makes a good insight?

As you build your powers of insight, remember to avoid falling into the confirmation bias trap that can hinder some researchers.

A good insight:

- Helps tell the story of the target audience
- Links people's needs and values
- Lets you develop criteria for a successful solution
- Serves as a foundation for the final human experience.

Sharing your insights with your team can be daunting. Remember you can always 'test' your insights by speaking to other experts or inviting people to share their reactions.

When you're ready to share your insights:

- Package your insights so they're easy to share – depending on how you share content at work, this may be a slide deck, web page, teleconference or printed report, or a mix of these
- Make it easy for your audience to follow the path of your insights from the raw data through to your well-formed conclusions
- Make sure your insights are memorable by giving your package or presentation a cool name. Use a short description that people can understand quickly
- Avoid buzzwords and jargon, as they can confuse or alienate people.

Evidence is essential

A fundamental principle of human-centred design is that it is evidence-based – insights from human-centred design must be able to be traced back to the research.

Designers and researchers must be able to articulate how they arrived at their insights. If they cannot do this, they are very likely allowing their biases and preconceived ideas to influence their decisions.

An example of what an insight is not

Drilling into the two diamonds

Let's take another look at the phases of the two diamonds. Here's a refresher:

- Diamond 1
    - **Discover** Also known as the research phase, where you gain insights into the problem or problems
    - **Define** Also known as synthesis, where you determine and articulate the problem you'll focus on
- Diamond 2
    - **Develop** (also known as *ideation*) Where potential solutions are developed and tested
    - **Deliver** The final phase, also known as *implementation*, when workable solutions are released to the users.

In the following sections, we explore the first diamond in detail (see Figure 12).

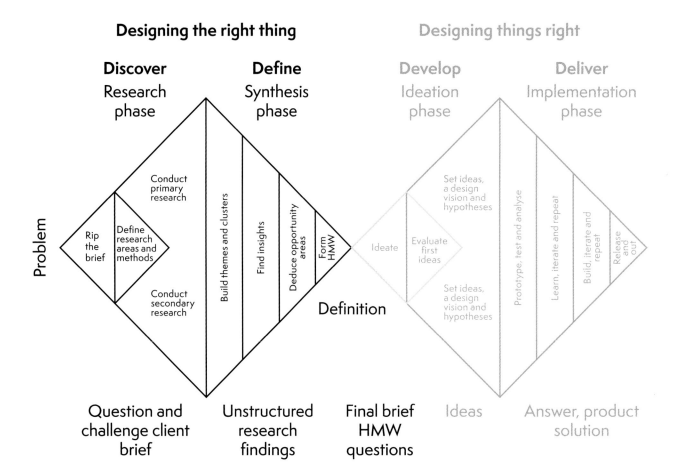

Figure 12 Diamond 1 – discover and define

Diamond 1, phase 1: Discover

Table 3 The discover phase

Thinking is mainly:	Divergent
Research is mainly:	Qualitative
Tools include:	Empathy map
	Site visits
	Contextual enquiry

The first diamond is where you'll start researching and using divergent thinking to gather all the data and insights you can.

The *discover activity* (see Figure 13) constitutes the research phase. Here we use divergent thinking to explore what the problem might really be. We throw away assumptions, think anew and embrace change. We focus on identifying, researching and understanding the user's problem. Remember: all sources of information are worth considering, so keep your focus wide.

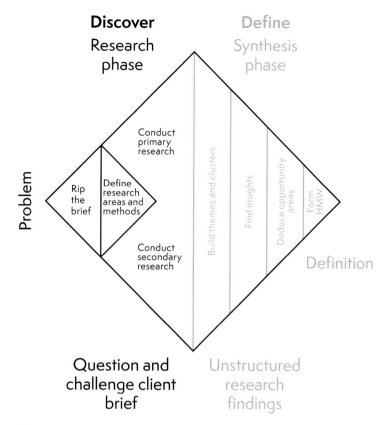

Figure 13 Diamond 1 – discover

The research tools you'll learn in this section will be valuable to you throughout the IT service design process. For this reason, we'll spend quite a fair amount of time talking about research – but remember, this book is not designed to provide the skills and knowledge that human-centred design demands, it's designed to help you start your journey into Humanising IT.

Remember that the discover activity is where we take the time to learn about the problem in detail. We throw out our assumptions about the people or the problems. We spend time with the humans we're designing for, and make sure to use a set of tools to listen, observe and empathise. Basically, we spend a lot of time in *divergent* thinking. The discover phase encourages us to use qualitative tools to gain an understanding, and to put our assumptions aside.

 Key message

Keep in mind that our goal is to eventually define the problem in specific detail, so we can deliver a solution that meets the actual problem – not our assumption of what the problem is.

Get to know your user

By now, you've read the sections about empathy and thought, 'Easy! All I've got to do is listen, observe, and ... what, exactly?' As an IT service management professional, you may fall into the trap of thinking you already know your user.

After all, isn't the user that person who phones you in a panic when they can't access their email, print their document or when their application has crashed? Or rings the service desk for a password reset – even though the IT department has created functionality for self-service? (Hmm, I wonder why users don't tend to use these self-service options? – OK, I'm being a little sarcastic here, but this sarcasm is founded on the number of poorly designed and convoluted self-service portals I have seen. It's no wonder users have a poor perception of IT and feel they have no other option than to call the service desk.)

Drop those assumptions! Let's take a look at a powerful tool for getting to know our user – the real user, not the faceless one at the end of the phone.

The empathy map

If empathy is sounding a little too, well, 'divergent' for you right now, here's a tool you'll love. An *empathy map* is a simple, digestible visualisation that captures your knowledge about a user's behaviours and attitudes. It lets you 'get inside the head' of the user, and then draw it. This can help you, as a designer, to quickly and easily understand the user.

Definition: Empathy map

'… is a collaborative visualisation used to articulate what we know about a particular type of user. It externalises knowledge about users in order to 1) create a shared understanding of user needs, and 2) aid in decision-making.'[52]

Empathy mapping is a simple workshop activity, and doesn't need a lot of time, energy or resource, with templates and guides readily and freely available online.

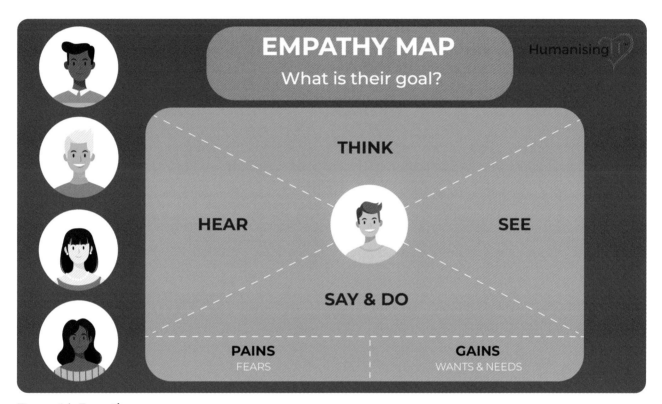

Figure 14 Empathy map

Empathy maps are most useful at the beginning of the design process – after user research, but before the more in-depth processes of requirement gathering and ideation.

Other techniques

There are lots of other great techniques used in human-centred design to undertake research, such as visiting the actual place of work and contextual inquiry. These techniques and much more will be covered in later publications in our Humanising IT series.

---

52   Nielsen Norman Group. Empathy mapping: The first step in design thinking. https://www.nngroup.com/articles/empathy-mapping/.

Diamond 1, phase 2: Define

Table 4 The define phase

Thinking is mainly:	Convergent
Research is mainly:	Qualitative, quantitative
Tools include:	Current state map

In the define phase (see Figure 15), we turn raw data into insights, narrow down the observations we've made in order to determine what is most relevant, and start to define a clear problem to solve. Here, we're focusing on the potentials of the user experience.

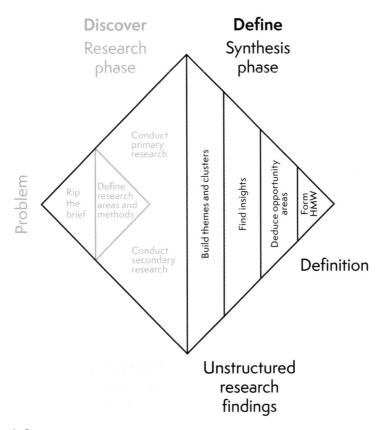

Figure 15 Diamond 1: define

This phase of the Double Diamond uses convergent thinking in an approach called *synthesis*. We're synthesising all our discoveries from the research so that we can create a definition of the problem that is as specific and clear as it can be. Your thorough understanding of the user's experience, motivations and priorities will help you to do this.

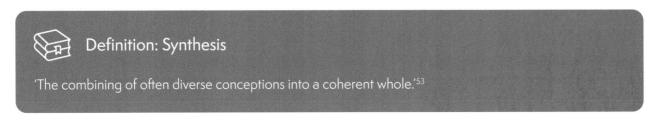

Definition: Synthesis

'The combining of often diverse conceptions into a coherent whole.'[53]

---

53   Merriam-Webster. https://www.merriam-webster.com/dictionary/synthesis.

The purpose of the define phase is to define the problem in detail and with specificity. This is called – unsurprisingly! – the *problem definition*.

By the time you complete the processes of the first diamond, you may feel that you're no closer to a solution. And in some ways, that's true: the first diamond is about exploration and challenge. It's not about solution: that's the work of the second diamond.

 Definition: Problem definition

A clear statement that outlines the problem, its negative impacts and why it matters.

Designers and researchers may synthesise and develop insights from their research, but the process of getting to a problem definition is actually collaborative.

Make sure the project sponsor or service owner is in agreement with you – you need to make sure that the customer or user insights and problems are balanced against the commercial objectives of the business. You also need to make sure that the stakeholders who have the biggest stake in your project are on board.

Current state map

You've collected all the insights you can from your site visits, contextual inquiries, empathy maps, interviews – any and all of the tools from phase 1. It's during the second phase of the first diamond that you can build a current state map.

The current state map is a key artefact of human-centred design. Mapping the current state lets you visually demonstrate how things are working now. Or how they're not working now. It's only once you know the current state that you're able to improve, plan or make changes. A current state map includes all the steps of a process, along with the roles, responsibilities and workflows.

 Definition: Current state map

'A current state map describes the high-level steps to make [a] product or provide a service from customer order or request, until delivery back to the customer. It reflects what's actually happening today, not what should or could happen. [...]

The order is to create the current state, then ideal state, then future state.'[54]

A current state map allows us to:

- Better understand how a process is currently performed
- Determine what happened before the process began, and what happens after it's complete
- Identify whether there are any approvals or regulatory requirements
- Determine whether there is anything missing from the current state that could impact upstream activities
- Detect any duplication of tasks or workflows.

---

54   BPI. Value stream map (Lean manufacturing and Six Sigma definitions).
        https://www.leansixsigmadefinition.com/glossary/value-stream-map.

Current state mapping is typically conducted via brainstorming and workshopping. Some of the guidelines for these workshops are to:

- Keep an open mind
- Be open to change
- Maintain a positive attitude
- Make sure everyone in the team participates
- Stay focused
- Don't leave in silent disagreement
- Practise mutual respect; don't interrupt
- Be honest
- Don't blame or judge – this is a blameless environment
- Leave rank at the door: one person = one voice, regardless of position.

On a personal level, my team members are huge fans of that final rule. If you're determined to leave rank at the door, make sure you warn everyone about the HiPPO syndrome.[55]

Wait a minute … HiPPO syndrome? *Highest Paid Person's Opinion.* Don't let the HiPPO trample all over your own insights, which you've carefully cultivated from your research.

HiPPO syndrome at play

HiPPO syndrome can also be the tendency to interpret higher-ranking people's opinions as decisions, or 'they must know best' even if they didn't intend it that way.

---

55 The HiPPO syndrome: humans can't reliably predict design effectiveness.
https://traveltekker.com/2012/07/11/think-you-can-effectivelyjudge-effective-user-experience-design-think-again/

Over to you

Have you experienced HiPPO syndrome in a workshop or meeting?

Now that you have an understanding of this term, how would you approach a situation where the HiPPO syndrome was knowingly or unknowingly being used?

A note on future state maps

In addition to creating a current state map, you are likely to need a future state map. This will show the steps you will need to take to complete the task after the process has been redesigned. A future state map should be a realistic representation of what the experience will become.[56]

Getting to the right problem

The good news is that once you reach your problem definition, you'll have a clear idea of the context, and a deeper and more complete understanding of the problem, its drivers and impacts throughout the user experience.

With the problem now clearly researched and defined (and agreed), we can now turn our attention to the second diamond.

So, take a breath. We're ready to move on to diamond 2! But before we do that, take a moment to read an intriguing and insightful case study about Professor Michael Buist, a highly respected and experienced intensive care specialist. Not only is it an astonishing and powerful narrative, but it also shows a positive perspective of how technology saved and continues to save lives.

Key message

Human-centred design emphasises that it's important to understand the problem thoroughly before attempting (or even considering) any solutions. This research and preparation are important! – no, paramount!

Don't be tempted to rely on the 'usual way of doing things' or decide to stop exploring every time someone tells you 'that's the way it's always been done'. And never assume that 'best practice' is the best or the only solution.

---

56   Business 2 Community. Can't get to future state without knowing current state.
       https://www.verizon.com/business/small-business-essentials/resources/as-part-of-your-journey-mapping-efforts-youll/.

Case study: Intensive care, with Professor Michael Buist

Professor Michael Buist

In Chapter 1, Mark Basham provided a narrative on the lack of culture definition in IT service management. I had the opportunity to interview Professor (then Doctor) Michael Buist in my podcast series Humanising IT.[57] At the end of this truly astonishing and powerful conversation, we wrote the case study below, where we learn how technology bypassed a less than desirable culture and continues to be instrumental in saving patients' lives – an intriguing and insightful read.

Dr Michael Buist is an intensive care specialist with a unique perspective from both sides of the hospital curtain, having himself almost died twice due to medical mishaps.

As a medical registrar he survived a lung tumour that went undiagnosed despite an X-ray. In 2008 a routine operation for appendicitis left him on the brink of death. A last-minute diagnosis from his obstetrician brother probably saved his life. Galvanised by these experiences, Dr Buist is now on a mission to reduce the number of unnecessary deaths in hospitals worldwide.

He freely admits that healthcare can be a dangerous business. Ten per cent of people entering hospital can expect to suffer an adverse event and of those, another ten per cent will die or experience a serious disability. As living proof of those statistics he's emerged as a world leader in the push to improve patient care with a range of thought-provoking ideas to reduce human error inside hospitals.

ABC Commercial[58]

Case study: A doctor on call

At Dandenong Hospital in Melbourne, Australia, a middle-aged male patient unexpectedly took a turn for the worse. Faithful to standard procedure, the attending nurse read the patient's vitals and called the on-duty junior doctor, who made appropriate medical interventions. Although the patient's vitals and readings technically would have promoted the case to crisis level – requiring specialist doctor intervention – the patient seemed to stabilise. Both the nurse and attending physician felt assured that the patient would recover soon and agreed to an additional check the next morning. However, less than 45 minutes later, the patient's health destabilised again and, despite their best attempts, the patient was lost moments later.

In the subsequent legal trial, the nurses and doctors involved in the tragedy were cross-examined and questioned as to why they made the decisions they did. The central question at play was: 'Why did no one simply call the crisis medical team?'

This was the relevant standard of care and policy of the hospital. One of the crisis specialist doctors on call was Dr Michael Buist, who testified that he was on call that day and would have readily responded if only he had been notified that the patient had reached crisis levels. But the call never came.

---

57   Podcast recording with Katrina Macdermid and Professor Michael Buist, 28 August 2020. Katrina Talks Humanising IT: Professor Michael Buist on Apple Podcasts.

58   ABC Library Sales. Australian story – Doctor in the house (Dr Michael Buist).
https://www.abc.net.au/austory/summer-series-edition---doctor-in-the-house/9172732.

Dr Buist – educating doctors during hospital ward visits

In the aftermath of the trial, this tragic story haunted Dr Buist, and he soon dedicated himself to ensuring that mistakes like these would never happen again. He had spent years in the healthcare industry and knew that its corporate culture was laden with layers of procedures that required attending nurses and physicians to go through multiple approvals and calls in order to move patients to appropriate care.

Often, these layers delayed urgently needed attention and were subject to the discretion of busy medical professionals on the ground. Many nurses and doctors dreaded the thought of having to hunt down higher-level doctors on call, and this part of the established culture added to the difficulties in cases like these.

The surprising solution that Dr Buist discovered came from the world of IT. With his team, he developed software that tracks patients' vitals and other relevant data from the hospital bed, and immediately notifies the appropriate doctors on call to intervene when certain thresholds are reached.

Sounds simple, right? But, as professionals in every field know, a simple solution to a problem is not always welcome when it involves changing a deeply ingrained culture. Dr Buist eventually found a hospital in the United Kingdom willing to partner with him. The application ignored and bypassed cultural issues that were putting patients' lives at risk – the results were astounding.

The trial showed doctors' performance improved from 66% to 98%, with a huge reduction in mortalities. From the custom user interface of the application (designed with feedback from nurses) to the ease of escalating patients to the appropriate specialist doctor, hospital staff embraced the use of the new application.

The number of hospitals using Dr Buist's application continues to grow – the future is much brighter for the healthcare industry, and most importantly, for patient care.

Diamond 2, phase 1: Develop

Table 5 The develop phase

Thinking is mainly:	Divergent, convergent
Research is mainly:	Qualitative, quantitative
Tools include:	Ideation
	Yes, and ...

This section provides a high-level overview of the second diamond and the design process within (see Figure 16). Don't fall into the trap of thinking the second diamond is less important than the first. On the contrary! The second diamond is where you develop and deliver your solutions. Here, we will only be discussing the concepts of ideation and testing.

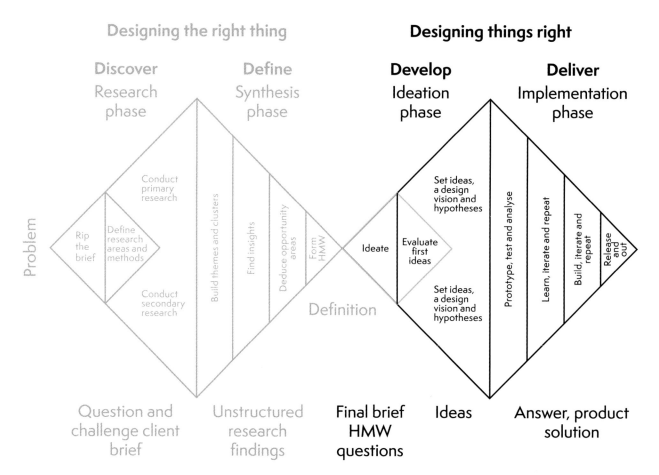

Figure 16 Diamond 2: develop and deliver

More on diamond 2

A detailed analysis of diamond 2 will be made available in further publications in our Humanising IT series.

Ideate, ideate, ideate

The term 'ideate' simply refers to the act of creating ideas. During the develop phase (see Figure 17), we create ideas for our potential solution. We explore multiple options. We challenge and test our ideas with different people. Not just the people who'll use our solution in their workplace, but the people designing and supporting the solution. That's right: IT people!

     Human-centred design for IT service management

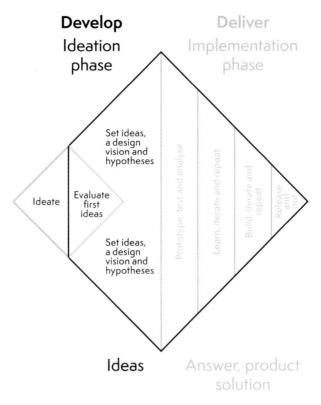

Figure 17 Diamond 2: develop

 Definition: Ideation

'... the *process of developing and conveying prescriptive ideas to others*, typically in a business setting. It describes the sequence of thoughts, from the original concept to implementation ... Ideation can be expressed in graphical, written or verbal terms.'[59] (italics ours)

Yes, and ...

So, how do we generate our ideas? We brainstorm, conduct workshops, interview. And ... we use the 'Yes, and ...' mindset.

'Yes, and ...' is a principle from improvisational comedy. It encourages improv artists to accept and expand on an idea their scene partner offers them.

- We're holding umbrellas? Yes, and ...
- We're in a submarine? Yes, and ...
- We're both fish now? Yes, and ...

'Yes, and ...' lets you move away from the idea-terminating mindsets of 'no' and 'that'll never work'. Remember, during divergent thinking, you're exploring and opening up possibilities. You're not trying to narrow in. That comes later, during convergent thinking.

---

59   Investopedia. Ideation. https://www.investopedia.com/terms/i/ideation.asp.

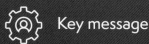

Key message

Use of the Double Diamond when designing is a highly collaborative team practice that works best when there's complete understanding and integration between team members. Ambitious? Maybe.

But you wouldn't be reading this book if you weren't ambitious, right?

At the end of the develop phase, you'll have an idea, or a shortlist of ideas, that you can consider carrying into the next phase. However, it is essential that you continue to involve all stakeholders to ensure that any ideas are feasible and viable.

Diamond 2, phase 2: Deliver

Table 6 The deliver phase

Thinking is mainly:	Convergent
Research is mainly:	Qualitative, quantitative
Tools include:	Wireframe
	Prototype

The next and final phase is where we move into the deliver activities (see Figure 18). Here we clearly articulate the solution we've chosen to solve the specific problem we defined at the end of the first diamond. We build, test, iterate, learn and repeat, until we feel confident we can finally release.

Test, you say? Yes: during this phase, testing is paramount. As we outlined above, we will be covering testing and other phases of the second diamond in later publications in our Humanising IT series. For now, you just need to know that the deliver phase asks you to test your solution with users. Testing doesn't require an entire build into a production environment: you can test with pen, paper and string.

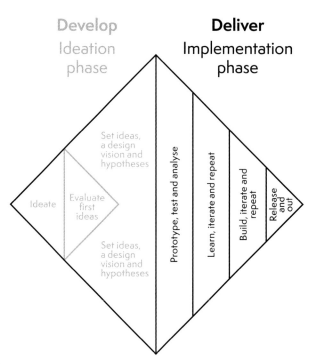

Figure 18 Diamond 2: deliver

User acceptance testing: an IT stalwart

User testing in human-centred design is about testing whether the person receiving your solution will actually use it, and how easy it is for them to use. It's not about testing the specific functionality and performance against the agreed scope and parameters of specifications.

This is quite different from the user acceptance testing typically performed by IT departments and requires a different mindset.

And the types of testing in this phase extend far beyond the testing typically performed within IT – the types of testing used by human-centred designers include *low-tech testing* and *proposition testing*.

For now, that's all we will be covering for the second diamond. But before we move on, we suggest you take another look at Figure 10, which gives a detailed view of the Double Diamond model: the phases, approaches and activities; it's a great artefact to refer to when designing.

Let's move onto another key concept of the Double Diamond: iteration.

Design is not a straight line

By now, you might be thinking that the phases of the Double Diamond look like a nice, linear progression from exploration and research through to delivery and implementation. Wrong!

Remember when we described the discover phase in the first diamond? In Chapter 4 (see 'It's not that straight'), we explored the Double Diamond and the IT value chains, and how both approaches are decidedly non-linear in the delivery and support of products and services.

Discovery can happen throughout the entire design process. To top it off, each phase can require several rounds of iteration before you can progress to the next phase. So, in truth, the Double Diamond model looks a little more like Figure 19.

 Key message

As we outlined in Chapter 4, there are activities you need to do in the right order. For example, you should never dive into ideation without research. You can't develop solutions if you don't know the real 'why' or have the insights on hand.

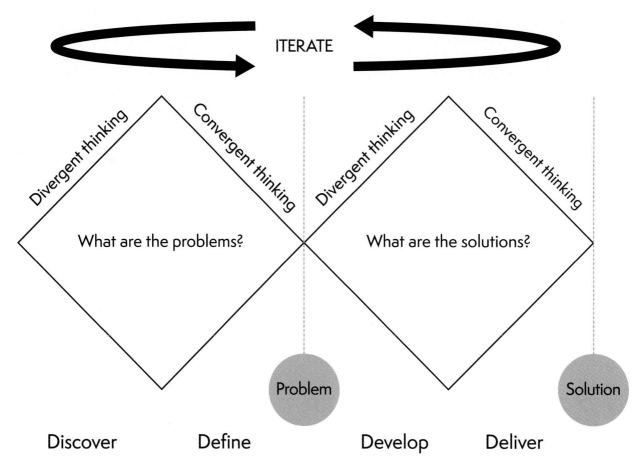

Figure 19 The Double Diamond illustrating the iteration for design

So, don't lose heart if you find yourself 'stuck in a loop'. No effort is ever wasted. Sooner or later, you'll have enough information to move forward into the next phase.

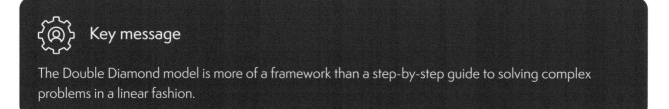

Key message

The Double Diamond model is more of a framework than a step-by-step guide to solving complex problems in a linear fashion.

The drilling has stopped, but our learning never does

That's it for our discussion on drilling into the Double Diamond – we've covered a tremendous amount and we hope you are continuing to see the benefits of integrating human-centred design into IT service management.

You can find a recap of this chapter below, but before reviewing our learnings let's take a moment to read an essay by Barry Anderson. Barry is a seasoned and experienced change advocate, and provides great insights into the importance of communication during any change initiative and the benefit of integrating human-centred design.

Barry has been responsible for transforming major organisations in both their culture and how they deliver customer experience. As Barry outlines, communication is key, and so is understanding the difference between what a transformation is and what an improvement is – these terms are often confused and misused! We do hope you enjoy Barry's essay.

Human-centred design and change initiatives

Barry Anderson – principal strategist

Human-centred design plays a critical role in driving and determining the success or failure of change initiatives

Standard strategic planning tools can help us to understand what the future will look like, and the scenarios created from analysis of likely futures can help us to understand the changed circumstances and the need for change to meet those circumstances. There are research methodologies and tools in abundance, but it is the stakeholder's perspective on their lived experience that counts, and this is where human-centred design is a key element of change.

Understanding both the changing environment and the lived experience of our stakeholders creates the bridge that allows us to relate strategic planning to the conduct of our change initiative. Human-centred design and understanding the stories of the lived experience of our stakeholders is what creates the greatest contextual value to those leading change initiatives.

The fundamental strategic questions for most organisations are: 'What does the future look like?' and 'What will my customers' expectations look like?'

We now have a much better educated and highly articulate community organised into special interest groups. Individually and collectively, they use high levels of expertise to define their expectations of very specific and highly targeted provision of services.

Human-centred design allows us to identify what will satisfy the expectations of these very vocal groups, and how we demonstrate that we have delivered on our promises. Have we actually realised the desired and valued benefits for our stakeholders?

As the APMG *Managing Benefits*[60] guidance points out, the delivery of benefits is not simply just one aspect of project and programme management, it is the rationale for the investment of taxpayers' and shareholders' funds in change initiatives.[61]

The wider the net is cast to engage stakeholders, the greater the prospects of meeting those demanded benefits. A common concern raised by organisations is the creation of stakeholder expectations that cannot be delivered upon. Genuine engagement of stakeholders using human-centred design enables organisations to clearly define those expectations in terms of outcomes required to be delivered. Stakeholders would usually prefer to settle for less, if that is achievable, than to seek to maximise benefits to the point of failure of the change initiative.

Scale of change

Implementing new strategies requires large-scale change within organisations. The term 'transformation' has emerged to differentiate the scale of the change initiatives driven by business strategy from the continuous improvement that organisations routinely perform.[62]

---

60   APMG accredits organisations to deliver training courses and consultancy services for a broad range of professional certification schemes. *Managing Benefits* consolidates existing guidance on benefits management into one place, while expanding on the specific practices and techniques aimed at optimising benefits realisation.

61   Steve Jenner. *Managing Benefits.* APMG International, TSO, London, 2013.

62   Robert S. Kaplan, David P. Norton. *The Strategy Focussed Organization: How Balanced Scorecard Companies Thrive in the New Business Environment.* Harvard Business School Publishing Corporation, 2001, pp. 331–332.

So how do we distinguish between business as usual (BAU), continuous improvement (CI) and transformation? Is it all the same, just bigger? Answer: 'No'.

BAU consists of the ways of working used by an organisation to achieve its (current) objectives in its steady state. Continuous improvement is a mindset driving the culture of performance-focused organisations to enhance their productivity beyond their BAU baseline 'steady state' activity using the existing resources and capability. David Kaplan sees continuous improvement as a mindset that seeks to break employees out of their complacency, where they believe that current performance is both good and adequate.[63] Transformation is a distinct strategic change to the way an organisation conducts all or part of its business.

But strategic impact is not the only critical differentiator; organisational capability is another. If you can use an existing capability to deliver the stakeholder outcomes desired, it is BAU or continuous improvement, not transformation. BAU and continuous improvement are about management and enhancement of the current BAU state, whereas transformation is about strategic leadership in response to significant changes, be they opportunities, risks or threats in the business environment.

John Kotter carefully distinguishes between the words 'management' and 'leadership' when describing transformation. 'Management is a set of processes that can keep a complicated system of people and technology running smoothly ... Leadership is a set of processes that creates organisations in the first place or adapts them to significantly changing circumstances ... Successful transformation is 70 to 90 percent leadership and only 10 to 30 percent management.'[64]

It is acknowledged by Henry Mintzberg that in management education, business as usual focuses upon the technical disciplines and technical specialisations required to maintain the status quo within the organisation.[65] It doesn't prepare people for leadership roles or for understanding the complexities of the world they will actually face. Preparing people for leadership roles is a critical value-add from early engagement with stakeholders, which is enhanced by the rigour of human-centred design. Collaborative engagement with others provides an understanding of all aspects of the business environment, which facilitates future problem-solving and systems thinking, providing a holistic view across the organisation.

Recap

In this chapter, we took a look at some of the tactical tools you can use to enhance the human-centred design process in your workplace. We examined ways of thinking (divergent and convergent), ways of researching (quantitative and qualitative) and a research trap (unconscious bias), along with some tips we've learned.

Then we worked with each diamond in the Double Diamond model, focusing on the discover and define phases in the first diamond and examining some of the tools you can use to define the problem, such as empathy mapping. We briefly discussed the concept of current state mapping.

Finally, we discussed testing techniques for your design process, and revisited the exciting concept that the design process isn't linear, it's iterative (but with certain guidelines to follow).

In the next chapter, we'll look at putting it all together with our unique Humanising IT approach to value streams.

---

63   Ibid.

64   John P. Kotter. *Leading Change*. Harvard Business School Press, Boston, 1996, pp. 25–26.

65   Henry Mintzberg. *Managers, Not MBAs: A Hard Look at the Soft Practice of Managing and Management Development*. Berrett-Koehler Publishers, 2004.

6 The new way to design value streams for IT

In this chapter, we will:

- Look at how IT service management is often too far removed from the customer to truly understand their experience
- Learn about value streams and value stream mapping
- Explore how IT service management value streams support business value streams
- Talk about Humanising IT service management value streams, and how we can design our IT service management to better serve and manage technology for our customers and users
- Learn the concept of service blueprinting and how this is applied to Humanising IT
- Introduce our unique three-layered approach to Humanising IT service management value streams.

Before we begin, a quick word (or two)

IT service management is often too far removed from the customer to truly understand their experience. So how can we understand their experience to design and support IT services?

By Humanising IT.

It's none of your business

How can you support your business if you don't truly understand what it does?

- How many hours a day does a database administrator employed by an airline spend talking to passengers on their planes?
- How many days a week does an IT change manager at a medical centre spend registering patients?
- How many times per year does a network engineer at a law firm meet the clients their firm represents?

If you answered 'none' to each of these questions, you're probably right.

As IT professionals, we're often acutely aware that there's a gap between our department and the people working in the client-facing side of the business. It's not the IT people who get to meet the passenger, patient or potential felon and understand their experience. It's the people interacting with the customers; it's the flight crew, nurses and lawyers whom IT professionals serve.

So the question becomes: 'If IT service management professionals have no business with the customers, how can IT service management *support* the business?'

Business relationship management

IT service management has a process called 'business relationship management'. As described below, the role is the conduit between IT and the business:

A business relationship manager (BRM) acts as a liaison between IT and other business units in the organization. As departments increasingly rely on technology, organizations often find they need to establish stronger communication between IT and outside business units.

The business relationship manager's role is typically a senior-level position, for which candidates need a wide range of experience, hard and soft skills and education to fill the job requirements.

As a BRM, you'll need a deep understanding of the IT department, but you'll also need the skills to effectively communicate with multiple business units and to understand their technological needs. You'll be a main point of contact between IT, HR, finance, marketing and other departments that rely heavily on technology for daily business.

CIO (IDG Communications)[66]

Wow – that's a hefty role, reserved for 'a senior-level position'. Forgive our gentle sarcasm, but perhaps there's a grain of truth in what we're saying too. It's not uncommon to hear senior IT people say things to their staff like, 'Don't talk to the business.' Or maybe you haven't been *explicitly* told not to talk to the business, but let's face it, IT professionals – especially operations people – are typically kept at an arm's length from business people.

In 'How to use this book', we highlighted that this book is not a replacement for specialist texts in human-centred design, but we have been able to introduce you to one of its key tenets (and arguably its foundation): *empathy.* By empathising with business users, we can create a great human experience, and in turn improve the relationship between business people and IT service management people.

In Chapter 1, we told you about the time John F. Kennedy met a janitor who told the then president that he was 'helping put a man on the moon'. The janitor understood the value of his role in the overall mission of the organisation.

But when we ask IT people what they do, we're often told:

- I write code
- I negotiate service level agreements
- I deploy the latest software patches.

---

66   CIO (IDG Communications). What is a business relationship manager? A key role for bridging the business–IT divide. https://www.cio.com/article/220098/what-is-a-business-relationship-manager-a-key-role-for-bridging-the-business-it-divide.html.

Very rarely do they say:

- I help customers board our planes
- I aid patients in receiving the correct medical advice
- I am instrumental in ensuring justice prevails.

Do IT professionals know what it's like to manage passengers when the boarding pass system isn't allowing passengers to board, and the flight's already behind schedule? Or to register a sick patient during a hectic morning when the phones won't stop ringing and there are murmurs in the media about a new pandemic? Or to wait on the outcomes of a forensics report when a software update has crashed the pathologist's database?

Those of us working in IT service management can find ourselves so distant from the customer's lived experience that it's difficult for us to empathise when designing our IT service management. In essence, that's what IT service management espouses to do: to *enable the business to meet the organisation's objectives and mission.*

 **Over to you**

How often in a week do you talk to a business user to empathise with their experience of IT services?

Does your IT department actively encourage you to spend time with other parts of the business? Do you have the opportunity to liaise with all senior levels in the business? If you answered yes to either of these questions, that is great, but typically IT professionals are not armed with the tools and techniques to enable them to understand the needs of users. So when, or if, you have an opportunity to spend time with other users in the business, it is paramount that the skills learned here are adopted to ensure that your IT service management properly considers and empathises with the needs of your users and colleagues.

Let's revisit some roles and introduce a story

Before we continue, let's revisit those roles – as a clear understanding is imperative for this chapter, and also for the Humanising IT approach to IT service management value streams.

 Definitions

- **Customer** The person deriving value from the business services.
  Alternatively: The customer is the person who consumes the organisation's business services, deriving value from what the business does (e.g. a passenger on a plane or a patient in a hospital).

- **User** The person using the technology to deliver value to the customer.
  Alternatively: The user is the person in the business who delivers a service to the customer. They might be someone requesting an IT service or requiring IT support (e.g. a newly onboarded employee or frontline staff).

Ultimately, in Humanising IT, the user isn't the person deriving the benefit from the service. They're *enabling the customer* to derive the benefit.

To further explain Humanising IT, we have created a story about a kitchen and a chef. Remember that storytelling is a key tenet of human-centred design (and something we believe should be used more widely in IT service management), and who doesn't love a good story?

> Stories are how people communicate; this is as true in design and business as in our personal lives.
>
> Hugh Graham Creative[67]

What's a restaurant without a kitchen?

Meet Saanvi Patel. She's a successful restaurateur with three thriving restaurants, and famous for providing an exceptional dining experience for her customers. She wants to ensure her vision is replicated across her three restaurants, even when she's not there.

Saanvi is meticulous and thorough. She works hard to establish the menu and ambience, and she sets the standards for service. At each of her restaurants, she's employed an accomplished chef to run the kitchen. It's the chef's job to provide a meal that's aligned to Saanvi's vision and standards, and to make sure the team adheres to all necessary compliance standards for the restaurant industry. The team members prepare and plate the meals to exacting standards.

Finally, it's the work of the waiters to deliver the food and beverages to the customers, meeting the high expectations that Saanvi's reputation invokes.

In this example, the people dining in Saanvi's restaurant are obviously the *customers*. The chefs provide services behind the scenes, much like the staff in an IT department. The waiters represent the business. They're the *users* – they're using the services provided by the chefs to deliver the experience to the customers.

Note that the chefs rarely go into the dining room to meet the customers. Despite that, their services in the kitchen are critical to the overall experience. You can't eat in a restaurant that has no kitchen.

Just like chefs, IT people rarely meet the customers. Of course, it's not entirely unknown for an IT person, or a chef, to leave the back rooms where their work is performed to do some work face to face. It's just rare.

Back to our story. The key to the exceptional dining experience in Saanvi's restaurants is the *collaboration* between the waiters and the chefs. Just like the key to delivering a successful business outcome that supports your organisation's mission is the collaboration between the business and IT service management.

Value streams and value stream mapping

We'll now explore the heart of Humanising IT: value streams and value stream mapping, and how they are adapted to IT service management in order to support business outcomes.

The concept of value streams and value stream mapping has been used for decades, primarily in manufacturing. Principally, value streams are about *action and value – supply and demand.*

---

67   Hugh Graham Creative. Story-centered design. http://hughgrahamcreative.com/2009/02/21/story-centered-design/.

Definition: Value stream

A value stream is a series of steps that occur to provide the product or service that customers want or need.[68]

There are many definitions of this term, but ultimately a value stream is a set of activities that creates value for the customer.

The origin of *value stream mapping* is often attributed to Toyota Motor Corporation and its adoption of the Lean methodology, which has a focus on continual improvement (Kaizen) and removal of waste.

Inside Toyota the practice was called 'material and information flow mapping' and was done almost as an afterthought. Toyota's success and use of lean manufacturing practices helped promote value stream mapping as a modern best practice for high efficiency business teams during the 1990s.

Atlassian[69]

Value stream maps, then, are a way to visualise the end-to-end activities that service providers and users are performing to create value for the customer together.

 Definition: Value stream map

A value stream map provides a structured visualisation of the key steps and corresponding data needed to understand and intelligently make improvements that optimise the entire process – not just one section at the expense of another.

Value stream mapping in IT service management

More recently, methodologies and frameworks have adopted value stream mapping for product and software development. They're also increasingly being used in business to understand the touchpoints of an end-to-end service, and demonstrate ownership of components, such as legislative obligations, governance and customer experience.

And yet, value stream mapping is rarely used within IT service management. True, there are some IT service management frameworks that use the concept of value stream mapping. However, in our opinion, value stream mapping remains a process-driven approach to IT service management, and doesn't include the entirety of the human experience of customers, users and the people designing and supporting the IT service.

---

68   Plutora. What is value stream mapping (VSM), benefits, process and value. https://www.plutora.com/blog/value-stream-mapping.

69   Atlassian. Value stream mapping. https://www.atlassian.com/continuous-delivery/principles/value-stream-mapping.

Examples of value streams in IT service management

Without being aware of it, IT service management uses some form of value streams, from restoring an incident to transitioning to a new service (but again, with little consideration of the experience). Here are the ones we've identified in Humanising IT:

- Issue to resolution
- Introduce to embed
- Request to fulfil
- Decommission to retire
- Detect to prevent
- Maintain to operate

At a high level, these six value streams are the most common ones in IT service management, but there are plenty more.

 Over to you

Can you identify three additional IT service management value streams that you use in IT service management?

In the Humanising IT approach to IT service management value stream mapping, we design our IT service management value streams to support business value streams. And business value streams support business outcomes, which – you guessed it – support your organisation's mission. Stay with us – it will all come together, we promise, and you're going to love our approach!

Revisiting the business outcomes of Fly First Airlines

We explored the business outcomes of Fly First Airlines in Chapter 1. To help us understand the Humanising IT approach to value streams, let's revisit some of the airline's business outcomes:

- On-time performance
- Consistent, timely and coordinated notifications of flight schedule and status changes to passengers and frontline staff
- Seamless onboarding from check-in to seating
- Accurate and optimised rosters available to manage crew operations
- All direct sales channels are available for bookings and payments.

---

70   Tim Stobierski (2020). What is a value chain analysis? 3 steps. https://online.hbs.edu/blog/post/what-is-value-chain-analysis

Now let's have a quick look at some of the business value streams at the airline:

- Check in passenger
- Board passenger
- Manage passenger baggage
- Provide lounge access
- Access, update and distribute the crew roster to the airport supervisor
- Upload flight schedules, including cancellations and delays.

Can you now clearly see how Humanising IT business value streams support business outcomes? And here's the clincher – *IT service management streams support business value streams.*

Now it's all starting to unfold. We can start to see and, most importantly, demonstrate the value IT brings to the business and how we, as IT professionals, support business outcomes. Let's explore that (because it's at the core of Humanising IT) with an example: rather than reporting to the business the number of incidents or percentage of problem tickets raised in a given month, in Humanising IT the IT service management value streams would allow you to report things such as:

- No flights delayed due to IT issues
- All passengers able to successfully print bag tags without error
- Crew optimisation systems available 24/7
- Online airfare sales increased by 18%.

And most importantly, you and your IT colleagues will actually understand what your business outcomes are – so you can design your IT service management to support the business's value streams and, of course, to ultimately support the organisation's mission.

Didn't we tell you that you're going to love Humanising IT and our approach to IT service management value stream mapping?

Processes in context and where is the 'why'?

OK, back to some boring stuff (but not for long). You are likely to be aware that processes have been the foundational 'safety net' in IT service management for decades. Many an IT department has been built based solely on processes, and has assigned roles, responsibilities and organisational structures based on processes.

An analogy

If processes were a book, they'd be a recipe book. They'd have clear instructions on how to create a cake from all the ingredients by following the step-by-step process through to the suggestion to 'serve with ice cream'.

Value streams would be more like a party planner, helping you get all the pieces together so your guest can celebrate a birthday or graduation.

Processes help us understand who does what, and in which order. What they often fail to tell us is the 'why'. If people don't fully understand the holistic view – *why they're doing what they're doing* – the process itself becomes everything. That way, processes can become dogmatic and weighed down by documentation. This can lead to processes that are inefficient, inflexible and unfit for purpose. In addition, opportunities for innovation may be ignored with the user experience or outcome not considered.

Just like in the example of Fordism we discussed in Chapter 2, employees may grow bored with rigid processes. They can lose motivation and satisfaction, often following processes for processes' sake, clocking off at the first opportunity, and dragging themselves in at the start of every day.

Sound familiar? Now you can see why too much structure in your processes can lead to a bloated, slow-moving system, resulting in dysfunctional and siloed ways of working in IT departments.

 Over to you

Does your IT department follow processes too rigidly with little ability to deviate?

Do your processes consider the user experience?

Do your processes consider the experience of IT professionals?

Would you describe your processes as efficient? If not, what impacts do these inefficiencies create?

It's about getting the balance right, right?

So, what's the solution? Retire all your processes and hope for the best? Of course not! Work that occurs without any process structure can lead to inconsistent outcomes, unpredictable work patterns and chaos. Ultimately, the answer is balance. And the only way to achieve balance is with a holistic mindset that focuses on the 'why'.

Why the 'why' is so important

As well as changing the traditional approach to IT service management (so that IT professionals truly understand the human experience of using IT services), there are two further benefits for an IT department when it adopts a human-centred approach:

- It's easy to see where IT service management aligns (or misaligns) with the business outcomes and what customers and users need – which means corrective action can be taken, if necessary
- Opportunities for improvement and innovation become more obvious and more welcome – allowing IT professionals to better partner with the business.

Human-centred design for IT service management

Key message

Processes often define the detailed activities for people to follow.

Value streams focus on the end-to-end view of how the activities (and processes) link together to create value for the customer and business.

The value of value stream mapping (and the 'why')

Value stream mapping enables you to build a *visual* flow of activities from demand right through to delivery, which makes it easier to communicate with people in and outside of your team, and to explain how value is being created. Most importantly, *value stream mapping helps you to explain why you do what you do.*

Value stream mapping also lets you redesign your IT service management processes by identifying:

- Waste
- Bottlenecks, gaps and backlogs
- Potential improvements, automations, streamlining and savings
- And, most importantly, how you can improve the experience – for all humans (including you).

 Key message

Value stream mapping helps us to understand what can be done better.

How long and how detailed does it need to be?

Value stream mapping can take as much or as little time as you have available. A value stream map can be a tool to quickly identify an improvement during a brainstorming session with your team – or it can be comprehensive and be an input for a major improvement or transformation. Depending on how much detail you need (or want), you can include systems and timings for each step, such as how long the step takes to perform and the lengths of the wait times between steps.

Let's take a look at a detailed value stream map, where wait times and comprehensive process flows are visualised. This example maps the production control for a manufacturing plant. Don't worry, our value stream maps aren't as detailed as the one shown in Figure 20 – we simply wanted to provide an example of the traditional approach to value stream mapping used in manufacturing.

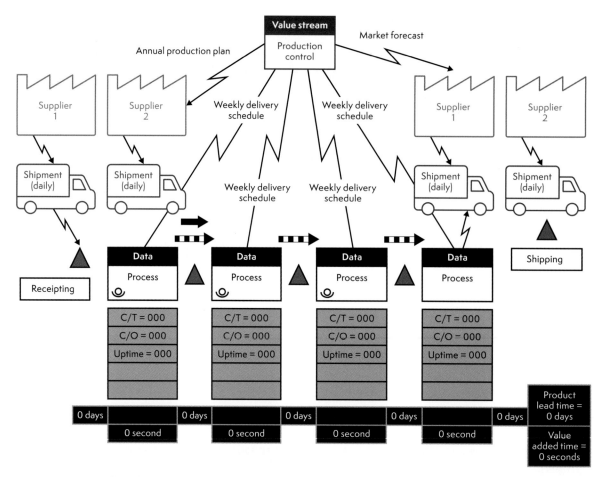

Figure 20 An example value stream map: production control
Adapted from www.slideteam.net

Business value streams and IT service management value streams

Given their origins in manufacturing, traditional value stream maps place the supply-and-demand mechanism, production control, at the top of the diagram. The original purpose was to ensure that production was as efficient as possible – not too much or too little passing through the manufacturing process. In Humanising IT value stream mapping, we place greater focus on business outcomes and how business people interact with customers. As you will discover, Humanising IT makes the customer journey the top layer of an IT service management value stream map.

Before we continue, let's clarify a couple of points. We've said that value stream maps are not in themselves a new concept. We've also discussed how the concept is now being used more widely outside of manufacturing – value stream maps may (or may not) identify the technology needed for the service or product. However, a value stream map typically does not show *how* the service will be designed and supported. Or, to put it another way: a typical value stream map does not include IT service management.

This means some questions can't be answered by your typical value stream map, such as:

- What skills are required for the support of the service?
- What is likely to go wrong with the service?
- How does the service get transitioned into operations or business as usual?
- What are the service levels?
- How do peak demand times impact the people in IT?

Key message

In Humanising IT, our approach is based on the premise that IT professionals don't directly engage with the customer who is receiving the value of a business outcome, making it difficult for them to understand why we do what we do.

Therefore, Humanising IT uses human-centred design to empathise with business users – because it's these users who have the relationship with the customers, and it's these users that IT professionals need to have direct contact with.

Happy and unhappy paths

As we outlined earlier, the concept of value stream mapping is not new, and the maps can have varying degrees of complexity and detail. They can also be depicted in many formats, including a customer journey map. We discuss customer journey maps a little later (and these are pivotal to Humanising IT) but for context, a customer journey map can be described as a visual representation of a customer's experience when using a service. Customer journey maps are typically created by human-centred designers working with digital and marketing teams.

A typical value stream (and in this context, a customer journey map) assumes a 'happy path' of how a service or product will be experienced; rarely does a value stream incorporate an 'unhappy path'. For example, a customer journey map might depict the great experience of a passenger using technology and all the stages to board a flight – but what happens when a bag tag is printed with the wrong destination for a passenger checking in? Like a recipe book, it doesn't tell us what to do if you burn the cake.

Gaining empathy by working with the business to define both 'happy paths' and 'unhappy paths' is part of the value and uniqueness of Humanising IT. But when human-centred designers create customer experiences using all the amazing tools and techniques we have learned, such as empathy, the Double Diamond and research, what they don't do (in my experience) is consider the IT service management complexity of designing and supporting the experience. Sure, they say, 'Yes, we do – we include tech', to which my response is, 'How are the tickets going to be logged between the suppliers supporting the experience?' Can you guess the response I get?

As we discussed in Chapter 4, integrating human-centred design with IT service management is not only paramount – in my opinion it needs to be mandated by CIOs, CTOs or any leader in an organisation responsible for customer experience (which should be all leaders). Both human-centred design and IT service management must work closely together, speak the same language and empathise with each other. Maybe my next book will be called *IT Service Management for Human-centred Design* – now there's a thought!

So, how can we be sure that the IT service management we're doing is valuable within a business value stream? Or better still, how can we be sure that IT service management has a seat at the table? That's where it's useful to distinguish between business value streams and *IT service management value streams*. In Humanising IT, we've built our own definitions of these terms.

In Humanising IT, we take a holistic view so that we can visualise the value of what we're doing in IT service management, helping us understand the 'why'. By understanding an organisation's business value streams, we can then design IT service management value streams that together create value to support the organisation's business outcomes and ultimately its mission.

Let's go back to our friends at Fly First. Earlier we explored the airline's business value streams, which might include:

- Check in passenger
- Board passenger
- Manage passenger baggage
- Provide lounge access.

Let's look at another industry: healthcare. A hospital's business value streams might include:

- Register patient
- Prepare patient for surgery
- Discharge patient.

And to recap, IT service management value streams typically include:

- Restore a service
- Fulfil a request from a user
- Retire a service
- Introduce a new service
- Detect issues to prevent a service outage
- Maintain a service.

Petra's peanut butter sandwich value stream – another story to tell

Let's look at a simple example using a home kitchen, and grab a taste of the Humanising IT concept to value streams in more detail. (You know how much we love a good story!)

Petra asks Dad for a peanut butter sandwich. This initiates the value stream where the customer (Petra) asks the business (Dad) for a specific service (make a peanut butter sandwich). The business value stream might be called 'Provide food'. Pretty simple so far.

Petra asking Dad for a sandwich

Petra asks for a peanut butter sandwich (demand) → Dad assembles bread → Dad applies peanut butter to bread → Dad assembles sandwich → Dad gives sandwich on a plate to Petra (value).

| Ask for sandwich | Receive request | Assemble sandwich | Deliver sandwich | Receive sandwich | Eat sandwich |

Figure 21 Sandwich value stream example

When Dad receives Petra's request, he goes to the kitchen to assemble and deliver the service (again, we mean he's going to make a peanut butter sandwich). The value is created when Petra consumes her sandwich and is then able to continue to play and grow. The sandwich value stream is shown in Figure 21.

What's happening in this example?

Notice that in the sandwich example, Dad is in the support role and Petra is the customer. Dad is supporting Petra's health and development by nourishing her in order to help her play and grow.

But let's bite a little deeper into this sandwich.

Dad goes to the refrigerator and realises the peanut butter jar is empty.

(Who left an empty jar in the fridge?!)

Dad finding an empty peanut butter jar

Dad immediately decides the perpetrator is probably Petra's brother, Barry.

Barry is at his regular skateboard meetup. So, Dad messages him and requests that he bring home some peanut butter, pronto!

Barry heading to the shop

Human-centred design for IT service management

Barry immediately takes a detour to the local shop. Going above and beyond the call of duty, he buys not one but two jars of peanut butter (crunchy *and* smooth), so he can be sure he's fulfilled the requirements. This makes Barry pretty similar to most of the IT departments we've worked in! Essentially, Barry is providing the IT service management. (We love Barry's proactive problem management!)

Barry purchasing the peanut butter

Barry gets home and proudly hands over two jars of peanut butter. Problem solved, according to Barry.

Then he has a long talk with Dad about his assumptions. No way did Barry leave that empty jar in the refrigerator.

(Why does he always get the blame?!)

Turning Petra's sandwich into value streams

In many ways, the saga of Petra's sandwich is directly relatable to our definition of IT service management value streams.

When an IT team has well-designed value streams, the result is more likely to be delivered on time, to expectations and in the most efficient way.

This means that in our example, Petra (the customer) knows what to expect when she puts in her request. Dad (the user) also knows what to expect from the services in the kitchen. But when he finds an empty peanut butter jar, there's a misalignment between what he (the user) expected and the service he received. Of course, he blames Barry (who's standing in for our poor, misjudged IT department).

Dad preparing Petra's sandwich

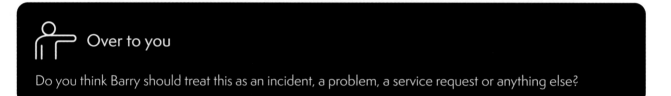

Over to you

Do you think Barry should treat this as an incident, a problem, a service request or anything else?

Dad providing Petra with her sandwich

Human-centred design for IT service management

Between them, Dad and Barry are delivering a service, and ideally they'd know:

- Which ingredients to use for a peanut butter sandwich
- How long the process takes to make a sandwich
- What skills are required to deliver the sandwich to the customer (Petra)
- What supplies are required
- When demand is likely to peak.

Dad knows what to do in order to deliver to Petra's expectations. He's the business. And Barry understands what's needed for the business to meet customer expectations. Just like an IT department.

Barry even went above and beyond in his service delivery by ensuring he could provide two different types of peanut butter. That's because he has a clear and holistic understanding of how the business (Dad) supports the customer (Petra). He understands the 'why'.

Barry's IT service management is pretty typical. There's a lot of background effort that goes into providing a service that meets customer expectations. Most of the time, Petra (the customer) doesn't know or need to know what activities her brother Barry (IT service management) is doing.

Just like an IT department, Barry understands what Dad (the business) needs to do to meet Petra's (the customer's) expectations

There's plenty for Barry to do, even during the moments when Dad isn't making sandwiches. Dad's agreed to pay Barry pocket money every week to look after the kitchen (hmmm – is Barry now a cost centre?). Now it's Barry's job to make sure the necessary supplies of bread and peanut butter are available. He must ensure he maintains a clean, accessible environment in which to make those sandwiches. And he needs the right tools to ensure Dad can meet his customer's expectations.

Petra with sandwich

In every organisation, IT service management is in the role of supporting the healthy functioning of its business – in other words, the business outcomes. And, just like in our simple sandwich analogy, part of the IT service management value stream occurs behind the scenes, making sure the business has everything it needs to deliver the final product or service – in other words, its outcomes – to support the organisation's mission.

 Key message

Value streams and value stream mapping essentially refer to the same concept. A map is just a visual representation of the stream.

Digesting the value stream concept

The reason why we enjoy food analogies throughout this book is that value streams offer a kind of recipe. In the example of Petra's sandwich, Dad and Barry have their own value streams. Dad knows how to fulfil the customer's request. Barry knows how to fulfil Dad's request.

Request to fulfil

Dad's request to Barry is an example of an IT service management stream that Humanising IT would label 'Request to fulfil'.

By mapping IT service management value streams – both the 'happy' and 'unhappy' paths that support business outcomes – IT professionals in collaboration with business people (users) can visualise and communicate how IT plays a pivotal role in supporting business value streams, which, remember, support business outcomes.

For example, Barry correctly identified that if he brought home two different types of peanut butter, Petra could have a choice of sandwich. And he could ensure there'd be enough *capacity* in the refrigerator and *availability* of the peanut butter supply to keep Petra eating sandwiches for weeks (don't you love how we throw in these IT metrics – capacity and availability?).

From Petra's point of view, much of the activity relating to her sandwich happens behind the scenes. Or, to extend the analogy, backstage. More on this later!

 Over to you

If we use the above analogy and the kitchen is the organisation – what do you think the mission of the organisation is?

Can you think of three business outcomes for the organisation?

What might three business value streams be?

What IT service management value stream would you design in case the refrigerator stops working?

So, what's missing from the value stream?

By itself, mapping the IT service management value stream is a great way to understand the activities required to deliver business value streams. Meanwhile, business value streams can identify the activities required to deliver value to the customer.

But they both lack a crucial element: the *human experience*. Value streams don't include human connection, emotion, creativity, relationships or – most importantly – the ability to empathise with our users and customers.

Value stream mapping alone doesn't encourage us to understand the needs and desires of the people we're delivering and supporting services to – nor does it understand the needs of the people designing the IT services that support the value streams. So, how do we improve our value streams? Simple: we humanise them.

Humanising IT service management value streams

So far, we've learned about the 'why' behind our approach to value streams. Humanising IT provides the method to demonstrate and communicate how IT professionals (i.e. people in the IT service management value stream) enable business outcomes (for people in the business value streams). In this sense, IT service management is empowering the business to create value for the customer, so it is an indirect relationship between the IT department and the value for the customers.

Let's look at *how* we humanise our value streams. The short answer is this: we empathise. When we empathise, we can start answering questions such as:

- Who are our users?
- What are their goals?
- What are their motivations and feelings?
- What are their expectations?
- What are their delights?
- What are their pain points?
- What are their pressures?
- What were they doing before/after consuming the service?

The answers to these questions provide key insights that we can integrate into our IT service management value streams – and this is where our previous learnings on the foundational concepts and techniques of human-centred design really start to come to life. Didn't we tell you that you would love Humanising IT?

 Key message

Remember that, as people working in IT service management, we can't necessarily determine or influence the business value streams. However, we can influence the points where we interact with the business to play a key role in enabling business outcomes – and of course, as we have learned, support the organisation's mission.

Let's look at some examples. As you read, keep in mind that we're focusing on improving how we, in IT service management, create value indirectly for the customer. Our role is to support business people – the users who play a pivotal role in supporting the customer-facing side of the business.

All the world's a stage

You've probably noticed that human-centred design loves a good analogy, and here we tell another story to help in our learning. To understand the next analogy, let's spend a night at the theatre.

Setting the scene

Here we are at the theatre, ready for a night of entertainment. The usher checks our tickets and directs us to our seats. Behind the curtain, the actors are preparing, the crew is moving props around, and the orchestra is tuning its instruments.

In this analogy, the customer experience is delivered on the stage. We call this the 'front stage' in human-centred design. Much of the activity required to deliver the customer experience happens behind the scenes, or in the 'backstage'. In Humanising IT, the backstage is where the IT service management activities largely happen. The IT service management staff make sure the equipment is running smoothly so that the people on the 'front stage' can do their jobs well.

But imagine if someone backstage turned out the lights at the wrong time (unscheduled maintenance) or closed the curtain in the middle of an act (unplanned outage) or didn't even know the performance hours (poor knowledge management).

The theatre analogy, using front stage and backstage, is a concept used by human-centred design

Coordinating the backstage and front stage activities results in a smooth and enjoyable performance that best meets customer expectations. Lack of coordination leads to a loss of harmony between the backstage and front stage. When this happens, the results can be disjointed or confused, and customer expectations are far from met.

Hit the lights!

What does this all mean? In this human-centred design analogy:

- The *front stage* is where the actors present the value
- The *backstage* includes the people and processes that ensure the actors have their props and the curtains are up in time, and any other enabling activities the audience doesn't see
- The *audience* includes our customers – they're the ones deriving the value
- The *actors* are presenting the value to the customers – they're on the front stage (most of the time). The actors represent the users
- The *props* are anything the actors interact with to present the value for the customers to consume.

Let's apply this concept to our friends at our fictitious company, Fly First Airlines:

- **Front stage** Frontline staff, e.g. check-in agents, cabin crew, chauffeurs and airport lounge staff
- **Props** Customer-facing products, e.g. baggage drop-off counter, booking systems and aircraft meals (including plates, cutlery and wine glasses)
- **Backstage** The staff who customers usually don't see, e.g. baggage handlers, flight crew, engineers, chefs and cleaners.

IT serving the business

Let's extend the front stage and backstage metaphor further and explore a typical IT service provided to the business. The front stage is analogous to the IT service desk – the service desk analyst is the actor, and her prop is the support ticket.

If the ticket can't be resolved by level-1 support, it's escalated and moves to the 'backstage' for resolution. The ticket (or prop) then returns to the front stage, when either a resolution is achieved, the hardware is delivered or the user is consulted for more information. *Any time you interact with a user, you're on the front stage.*

So, how do the backstage people make sure they're supporting the front-stage actors to provide a performance that the audience can appreciate? In other words: how can IT service management better work with the business (users) to help deliver value to its customers and meet (or exceed) expectations? To answer that question, let's look at some other human-centred design concepts: the *customer journey map* and the *service blueprint*.

Customer journey maps: stepping into the customer's shoes

Let's spend some more time with Petra and her taste for sandwiches. She's hungry (again!) and asks Dad for a peanut butter sandwich. Dad delivers the sandwich, and Petra eats it.

Note that in this quick summary, we haven't included the full value stream. When Dad receives Petra's request, he's on the front stage (in our analogy). When he delivers the sandwich, he's again on the front stage. Any time he interacts with his customer, he's on the front stage. But when he's making the sandwich, checking the peanut butter supply, or interacting with Barry to get more peanut butter, he's backstage.

For now, let's stay with Petra's experience and take a look at her customer journey.

> **Definition: Customer journey map**
>
> 'Customer journey maps are used to map the relationship between a customer and an organization over time and across all channels on which they interact with the business. Design teams use customer journey maps to see how customer experiences meet customers' expectations and find areas where they need to improve designs.'[71]

The customer journey map answers questions such as:

- What are the customer's key goals?
- What is the customer's experience of our business service?
- How long does the customer have to wait from beginning to the end of the process?
- Where is the customer coming from and where are they going?
- What was the customer doing before and after?

---

71   Interaction Design Foundation. What are customer journey maps?
     https://www.interaction-design.org/literature/topics/customer-journey-map.

- What pressure is the customer facing while waiting for the final value?
- What actions are they taking?
- What things are they interacting with?

A customer journey map paints a picture from the customer's perspective that describes their experience of interacting with the organisation. Customer journey maps have a unique beginning: they don't start when the customer starts interacting with the service provider. They start just before that, when the customer's need first arises, or when they first consider which organisation to approach.

 Key message

The customer journey is compiled after research; it's backed by data, evidence, observations and interviews with all stakeholders (not only the customer).

Let's build a simple customer journey map for Petra now – this is illustrated in Figure 22.

Figure 22 Petra's request for a sandwich: a customer journey map

Note how in this attempt of visualising Petra's request for a sandwich, we start with what Petra was doing immediately before she asked for a sandwich: playing in the park. She then realised she was hungry, so she asked for a sandwich.

Customer journey maps do more than identify a series of steps – that is what a value stream does. In Humanising IT, we use this technique to complement IT service value streams in order to gain insights into business users' motivations, desires and expectations – before, during and after they come into contact with IT. Humanising IT offers the opportunity for IT professionals to gain a profound level of user knowledge and empathy (including users' emotions) that goes beyond the typical and traditional interactions of IT and the business.

 Key message

In a customer journey map, the human experience is at the heart of its creation.

Let's visit our friends at Fly First again to gain a deep understanding of this concept and see how a customer journey map might be used for mapping a passenger persona, called Lucian.

Lucian's flying home to see a loved one – he hasn't seen him for over two years. What is important to note is that the customer journey map includes Lucian's actions – before, during and after the flight. And of equal importance is his *emotional* journey.

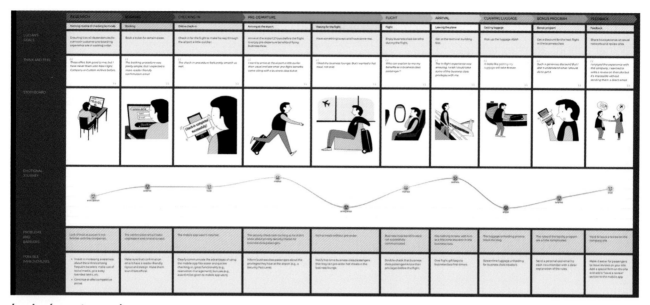

Lucian's customer journey map
Reproduced courtesy of UXPressia

Let's zoom in a little on Lucian – we can see him researching and checking in for his flight. We can see the storyboard of his actions, his touchpoints, what he is thinking and feeling, and his emotional journey.

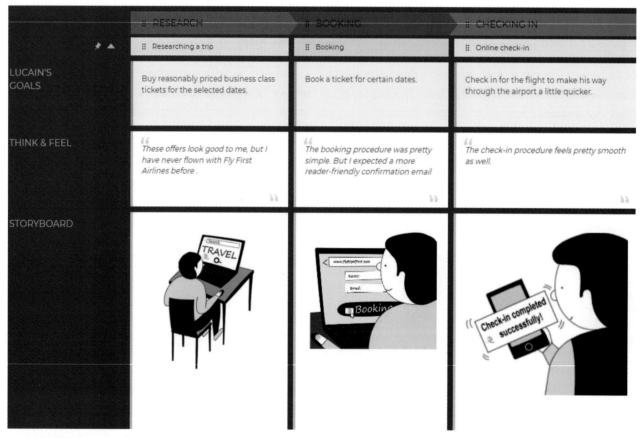

	RESEARCH	BOOKING	CHECKING IN
	Researching a trip	Booking	Online check-in
LUCAIN'S GOALS	Buy reasonably priced business class tickets for the selected dates.	Book a ticket for certain dates.	Check in for the flight to make his way through the airport a little quicker.
THINK & FEEL	*These offers look good to me, but I have never flown with Fly First Airlines before .*	*The booking procedure was pretty simple. But I expected a more reader-friendly confirmation email*	*The check-in procedure feels pretty smooth as well.*
STORYBOARD			

Detail of first part of Lucian's customer journey
Reproduced courtesy of UXPressia

Human-centred design for IT service management

Customer journey map

At its most basic level, the customer journey map (see Figure 23) situates the business *interaction* within the context of the overall trajectory of the customer as they go about addressing their needs and desires.

In its more complex versions, a customer journey map can utilise precise analytics and AI systems to depict a much more detailed image of the customer experience.

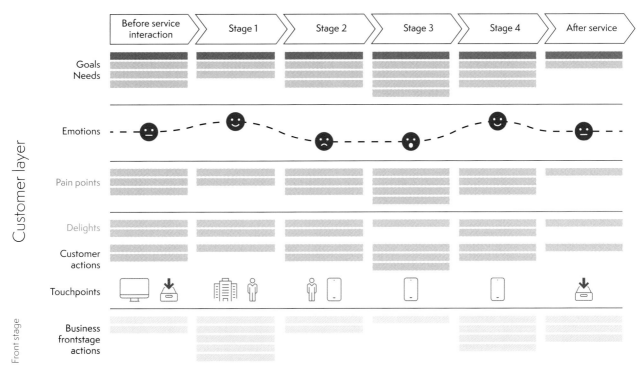

Figure 23 Template example: customer journey map

I especially like the following quote – I believe it reflects and, in many ways, epitomises how KPIs are assigned to IT departments and measured per group or team, without fully understanding (or empathising with) the entire experience of our users.

Journey mapping combines two powerful instruments: storytelling and visualization.

Storytelling and visualization are essential facets of journey mapping because they are effective mechanisms for conveying information in a way that is memorable, concise and that creates a shared vision. Fragmented understanding is chronic in organizations where KPIs are assigned and measured per individual department or group because many organizations do not ever piece together the entire experience from the user's standpoint. This shared vision is a critical aim of journey mapping, because without it, agreement on how to improve customer experience would never take place.

Nielsen Norman Group[72]

The elements in Table 7 are common when designing customer journeys, but some may not always be relevant. Include each element as needed for your journey.

---

72   Nielsen Norman Group. When and how to create customer journey maps.
      https://www.nngroup.com/articles/customer-journey-mapping.

Table 7 Key elements and techniques of a customer journey map

Element	Notes
Customer language	Ensure the journey map is written in the voice of the customers and represents what your customer would actually say, feel, want and do – not business language, and definitely not IT or technical language
Goals (not just one goal)	It's important to note that there will be all kinds of goals, not just one. You need to include the overarching one, and the ones at each step of the journey (where relevant). If we look at a passenger from our friends at Fly First Airlines – the overall goal and the various goals for steps within the customer journey might be: • Overall goal – Go on holiday / get to my destination • Airport goal – get to the right gate on time with everything I need • Check-in goal – get my boarding pass and drop my baggage off
Sequence	Sequence the phases or steps that the customer needs to take to achieve their goal
Emotions	How positive or negative is the customer feeling at the different stages? Depict the emotions as a graph from positive to negative, and use descriptive words: excited, apprehensive, frustrated – any emotion that is relevant should be applied
Pain points	Identify things that cause issues and frustrations for the customer at each step
Customer actions	The choices, steps and activities that the customer is undertaking as they move towards their goal
Touchpoints	In practical terms, touchpoints are the tangible elements of the service: physical or digital objects, such as a receipt or boarding pass. Further examples of touchpoints include a self-service kiosk, an ATM, an app on a smartphone, a website or even when speaking with a call centre – the touchpoint would be the telephone. And, in the case of a traditional check-in at an airport, it would be the counter; some might argue that even the customer service agent is a touchpoint
Interactions	An interaction is a moment within the journey – it's a place and time in which the customer experiences the service. This might include exploring an airline's website and comparing the prices of different flights. Other interactions might be the transition from comparing the prices to purchasing a ticket, or consuming a meal onboard the aircraft. It may be simpler to think of interactions as moments in which information is exchanged or the customer transitions from one step into the next. It's also important to depict moments when a customer is waiting or considering the best option
Channels	Channels are defined by the way in which customers receive the information or experience the service. For example, digital channels include smartphone apps and websites

As we explored earlier, in our first example of our value stream mapping for Petra's sandwich, we didn't capture what she was thinking or feeling, what she was doing before she asked for the sandwich, what delighted her, and what motivated her to ask for, say, peanut butter instead of jam.

But a customer journey map allows us to include all those things. We can map other feelings, like her delight at eating in the park, or her impatience at being made to wait for Dad to return with the sandwich. We can better understand her motivations, emotions and expectations.

Why does this matter? All of this helps us empathise with Petra and design an experience that will – hopefully – delight her and support Dad's business outcomes.

Let's now line up Petra's customer journey with the activities that are happening backstage in order to deliver her experience. We do this by building a service blueprint. What's a service blueprint? Great question …

Key message

Although Humanising IT focuses on the journeys of the user and IT professional, ultimately organisations exist to deliver value to customers; therefore it's important to understand the customer journey.

We recommend is that you speak to your digital team – they will more than likely have created customer journeys (and this is a bug bear with me as these are not typically shared with IT professionals). If your company does not have a digital team, we strongly urge you to work with the business to create customer journey maps against the most common business value streams within your organisation.

Service blueprints

A service blueprint includes all the relationships and interactions that happen between the customer, the different parts of an organisation and its partners. By exposing the 'big picture' and all the interactions that take place, it can become easier to understand the impact of activities or design that might not have been considered. For example, incorrect data capture at the beginning of a business value stream might have a downstream impact.

Key message

A service blueprint can be described as 'part two' of the customer journey map.

Let's look at this example a little deeper and visit our friends at Fly First Airlines once more. One part of the business owns the check-in and auto bag drop service – allowing passengers to check in both themselves and their baggage. Another part is focused on ensuring that passengers can book flights. If issues arise with how customer data is captured during the booking activity, there can be downstream issues impacting the ability of the other team to ensure that the check-in service functions.

What would happen to passengers like Brad and Jen when they checked in if the auto bag drop service didn't record their number of bags correctly? The baggage handlers may not be able to safely determine how much space or 'load' is available on the aircraft. Conversely, if the check-in service didn't record that Brad and Jen are travelling together, seat allocation would more than likely be compromised.

Who is service blueprinting for?

Service blueprinting is best for complex services – for organisations that are best described as eco-systems rather than just production lines.

Service blueprinting is ideal for organisations that deliver services across different channels or physical sites like airports and bank branches, and that have digital products such as apps and websites.

Definition: Service blueprint

A service blueprint includes a visual representation of the steps a customer goes through as they experience the service, known as the 'customer journey'.

We then also include all the *backstage activities* that the organisation and partners need to complete in order to support the front-stage or customer journey.

The different components of the service – people, places, processes, props (digital or physical) and capabilities – are laid out in a sequence of interactions or touchpoints. These interactions occur on the front stage, above what we call the *line of interaction*.

Definition: Line of interaction

Separates the interactions the customer has with the business. Everything the customer can touch and see, such as a website or service agent, is above the line of interaction on the 'front stage'. Everything that's hidden from the customer (the things they don't see or interact with) is below the line, in the backstage. The intersection between the two is the line of interaction.

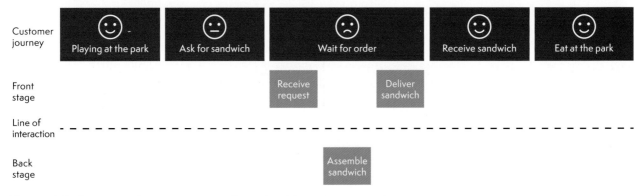

Figure 24 Customer journey map and service blueprint example

Note that in the service blueprint in Figure 24, Dad is only interacting with Petra on the front stage. His backstage activities occur below the line of interaction.

Key message

Adding the backstage elements is what turns a simple customer journey into a service blueprint.

With Petra's sandwich, there are activities that occur front stage and backstage. Remember that the front stage is where the interactions with the customer occur: Dad receives the request, and he delivers the sandwich. Also on the front stage, Dad uses several props, such as the plate the sandwich is delivered on. Backstage is the kitchen where Dad makes the sandwich. Once we've included backstage activities in our visualisation, we've created a service blueprint (see Figure 25).

It could be said that the service blueprint is a higher-resolution visualisation of how organisations and customers co-create value. Service blueprints provide more detail than the simple value stream and customer journey maps we saw earlier. But something's still missing.

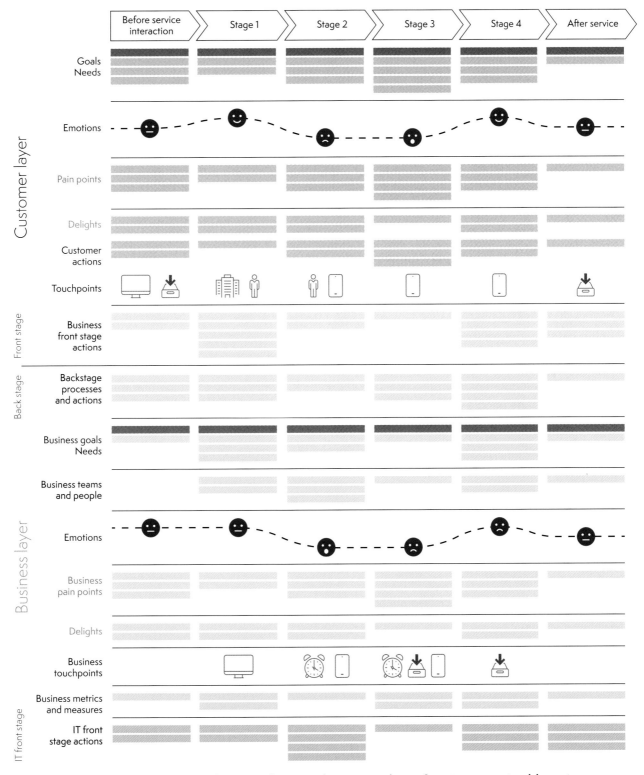

Figure 25 Template example: the business layer and customer layer forming a service blueprint

Addressing that empty peanut butter jar

Remember that Dad opened the refrigerator and realised the peanut butter jar was empty. Dad messaged Barry and asked him to buy some more peanut butter.

As we outlined earlier, Dad represents the business, fulfilling the customer's (Petra's) need. Barry is IT service management. He's enabling the business to provide services to the customer. Barry's contribution is key to enabling the outcome for Dad, but from Petra's point of view, Barry's activities are backstage. Barry has a different line of interaction: he doesn't interact with Petra (not this time, anyhow!), but he does interact with Dad. This means we need a new line of interaction and some new layers for our service blueprint.

And this is perhaps the most important component of Humanising IT – we include everyone's experiences, not just those of the customers. *We also include our IT service management people.* That's right: Barry's day has come at last.

The real star of the show

So far, we've looked at human-centred design tools and techniques to better understand and empathise with customers. Then we added the user's activities that enable the customer's outcome. What we haven't done so far is empathise with the user. And we haven't shone a spotlight on Barry's contribution. Let's do that now; this is what Humanising IT is all about.

Empathy for the customer, the user and for IT professionals

When Barry empathises with Dad, he understands that Dad already has a busy role. Before Petra asked for a sandwich, Dad was prepping for a weekend barbecue. When he receives Petra's request, he's already stressed and needs to deliver the sandwich quickly.

In Humanising IT, we map all the activities that Barry performs from an IT service management perspective – we map how Barry feels, what motivates him, delights him – in other words, we empathise with him. Barry's activities might include people, tooling, applications, service level agreements and, of course, processes that support the business value stream.

Before we move on, let's review the most common IT service management value streams we have defined in Humanising IT:

- Restore a service
- Fulfil a request from a user
- Retire a service
- Introduce a new service
- Detect issues to prevent a service degradation
- Maintain a service.

 Key message

Remember that empathising with the user and IT professionals is where Humanising IT differs from conventional customer journey maps and service blueprinting: although ultimately, when we are creating value for the customer, we are empathising with the user and IT professionals – not just the customer.

This empathy for the user enables IT service management staff to develop a greater sense of closeness and understanding for their colleagues in the organisation. This means we can design and deliver IT service management value streams that meet *their* expectations and, of equal importance, ours also.

Think about it. If your IT team had increased knowledge of and clarity of your business users' motivations, desires and expectations, it would largely benefit your ability to create value for them.

 Over to you

What do you think are the biggest pain points and delights for users of your IT services?

What do you think are the biggest pain points and delights for IT professionals?

How can you visualise these experiences?

How can you test your ideas?

What else can you do to practise empathy for the business user in your organisation?

What else can you do to practise empathy for the IT professionals in your organisation?

Adding an extra line of interaction between business users and IT service management enables IT professionals to understand the 'why' behind what we do, and our ability to support business outcomes to achieve the organisation's mission. Figure 26 includes the IT service management layer in the service blueprint.

 Over to you

Earlier in this chapter, we asked you to identify some business value streams in your organisation.

What benefits can you identify for your IT department if you were better able to understand and map the user experience in your organisation?

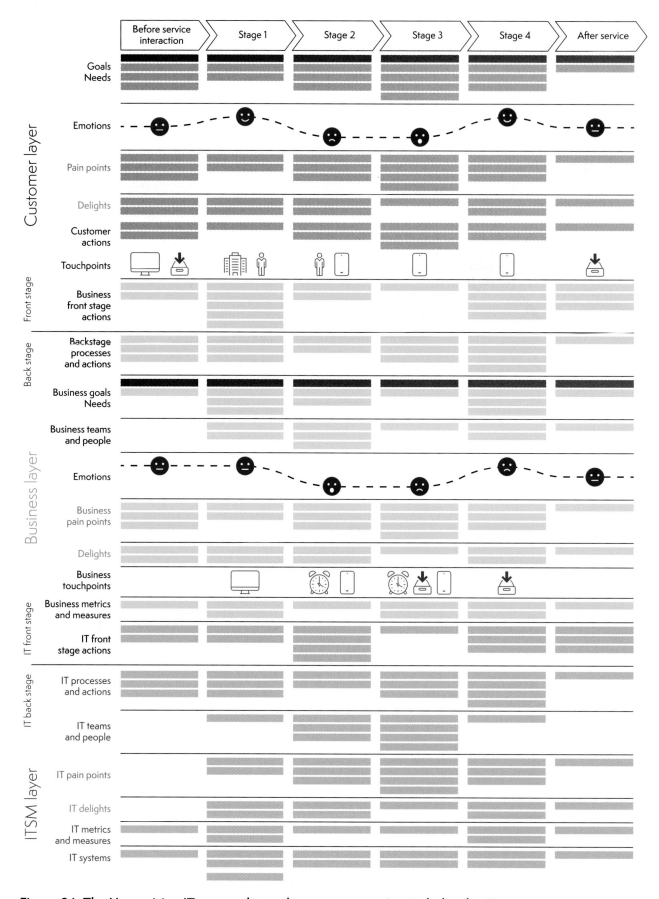

Figure 26 The Humanising IT approach to value stream mapping includes the IT service management (ITSM) layer

Human-centred design for IT service management

The IT service management layer

And here is the IT service management layer! Remember that it's not IT service management's job to design, influence or dictate the customer journey, but everything that IT service management does (or does not do) has an impact on the customer – either directly or indirectly.

Adding another line of interaction

To recap, in Humanising IT value stream mapping, we use two lines of interaction, whereas the standard service blueprint uses only one.

We visualise and humanise the interactions between business people – our users – and the IT professionals within IT service management. These lines separate the customer and business layers, and the business and IT service management layers.

Essentially, what we're doing with our approach to service blueprints is visualising the business value streams and IT service management value streams, and how they interact to support the users – which, of course, ultimately supports the customer.

As we have discussed, the issue we face is that the further away from the customer we are, the further we are from being able to deliver value. It is, however, important that IT service management doesn't place its own people and processes at the top layer (although we are still included) – ultimately organisations exist to deliver value to customers.

What is important and unique about Humanising IT value stream mapping is that once we understand the customer journey, we can map how the business (users) supports its business value streams. We can then map the IT service management value streams that support the business (users) in delivering value to customers.

In summary, Humanising IT creates three value streams:

- Customer layer
- Business layer
- IT service management layer.

 Key message

Humanising IT can also help IT professionals to identify:

- Inefficiencies in IT service management processes – do we really need to do that part of the process?
- Improvements in user experience – does the user really want to be contacted three times before we can close a ticket?
- Where gaps exist between the business and its IT services which impact the value being delivered. Why don't we build integration between two systems?

And much more!

Figure 27 Template example illustrating the capture of IT service management pain points and delights

In Humanising IT, we map the humans involved, including IT professionals. So we don't just ask the following questions of our users:

- What are their emotions when they need to wait a long time for an incident to be resolved?
- What are their pain points when receiving sub-optimal service from the IT service desk?
- What are their delights when interacting with IT?

Instead, as Figure 27 illustrates, when designing IT service management streams, we *also* ask the same or similar questions to IT service management professionals:

- How do they feel when there is a long call wait time for users?
- How do they feel when they know they are delivering a sub-optimal service to users?
- What are their delights when assisting users?

> **IT strategy = business strategy?**
>
> Did you know that both IT and business professionals alike are starting to say that 'the IT strategy is business strategy'? Interesting statement – but's that another book!

What we are saying is we need to empathise not only with the people we serve, but also with the people *who* serve!

We are nearing the end of our show

As IT professionals, what can we do with this additional information? The benefits of integrating human-centred design into IT service management go beyond internal team development. Humanising IT also allows us to make operational adjustments based on greater awareness of the customer experience.

As we have explored, understanding and empathising with how our users work, where they work, their pain points and all the other considerations we have learned in Humanising IT will allow us to create a better way of restoring a service or fulfilling a request. Equally and importantly, we empathise not just with users but with ourselves – IT professionals – and, at the core of it, this is what Humanising IT is all about.

On the interpersonal level, our approach alone can greatly improve a company's culture of respect and mutual understanding and start addressing those issues we discussed in Chapter 1. Do you remember the section in Chapter 1 where we asked IT professionals, 'How do the business people describe your IT department?' Again, you may recall the most common responses: complicated, slow and expensive.

Humanising IT allows you proactively engage with the business to identify opportunities to contribute to – or even enhance – business outcomes and contribute to the organisation's mission.

This is only the beginning of our exploration of what IT service management can learn from human-centred design.

And we're near the end of the book, but not of the journey

Humanising IT demonstrates we can design better IT service management value streams by integrating human-centred design and challenging traditional IT service management.

And, just like the janitor who saw the part his role played in putting a man on the moon, Humanising IT paves the way for all IT professionals to have a clear understanding of their integral role in supporting the organisation's mission.

We hope you have loved learning how you, as an IT professional, can design and support IT services that your users will love and your colleagues will love – by putting humans first.

That is Humanising IT.

Katrina Macdermid

7   Integrating human-centred design into IT service management – a case study

Welcome to our complementary chapter in Humanising IT.

Up to this point, we have reviewed some theory, examined insights and provided examples on how to integrate human-centred design into IT service management. In this chapter we look at a fictitious (but very relatable) scenario within the IT department at Fly First Airlines. At the end of the scenario, we will ask you some questions. Using your newly acquired skills obtained while studying Humanising IT, consider your approaches to the questions posed – and, most importantly – how your responses would support Fly First's business outcomes to meet the airline's mission.

Let's start learning more about Fly First Airlines and its people.

Fly First Airlines

Founded in 1982, Fly First Airlines is both an iconic and a symbolic airline for many Australians. Widely recognised for its impeccable safety record and premium service, Fly First's main business is flying passengers. The airline plays a vital role in the transport of tourists to and around Australia. Combining the contribution of both domestic and international tourism, it is estimated that the airline annually contributes over AU$8 billion to the Australian economy.

Domestically the airline operates over 400 flights and transports over 200,000 passengers daily. Fly First, through its code-sharing programme, can offer passengers a wide range of global destinations, allowing them to travel beyond the Fly First network. This dispersed presence of Fly First has made it a truly global corporation.

Fly First's headquarters are located in Melbourne, and it has offices in the Pacific, Asia, the US, Europe, Africa and the Middle East. The airline employs over 20,000 staff. Fly First is the sum of its skilled, passionate and diverse workforce.

A sense of pride and ownership is prevalent among the airline's employees, which is reinforced by the company's brand values: 'An airline that is us' and 'Fly First, that's what we do'. The airline boasts a harmonious workforce, and its people comprise airline crew, ground handlers, corporate office staff, meteorologists, chefs and doctors. The airline employs people from around the globe, creating a multi-cultural environment that fosters respect and teamwork. The leadership team takes culture seriously and firmly believes that a satisfied workforce contributes to the airline's number one priority – safety and the well-being of both passengers and staff.

Message from the CEO

'We are committed to building and fostering a culture in which diversity is valued, and to providing a workplace that is free from discrimination, harassment and bullying.'

Scenario – Fly First Airlines bag tag issue

We met Carmen earlier when we discussed personas – you may recall that she is the airport supervisor at Fly First's busiest airport: Sydney, Australia. As we discovered, Carmen has a passion for the aviation industry, and that zeal extends to her passengers. To Carmen, a great day means that her passengers and her team are happy.

Walking between the check-in and the auto bag drop counters early one Monday morning, Carmen is approached by an anxious passenger. The counter used by the passenger has printed a bag tag with the wrong destination. It seems that the passenger will be flying to Rome, but their bag is going to Hawaii. This is an issue that has a high impact on both passengers and airport staff, and crucially, is also of high impact for baggage handling – a core service of the airline. Carmen immediately places an 'out of order' sign on the counter and reaches for the shared mobile phone to call the IT service desk at Fly First. She wants to get this issue resolved quickly before the morning peak hour.

Ticket is logged

Her call is answered by Sue. There was a software update to Microsoft Windows over the weekend, resulting in most users not being able to access their applications. As a result, the IT service desk is being inundated with calls, emails and chats.

Sue has worked on the IT service desk at Fly First for just under a year. Her dream is to travel the world and she sees this role as a stepping stone to realising her dream. Sue logs a ticket on Carmen's behalf, and obtains the initial information required by the incident management process. So far, there's only one impacted passenger. Based on Fly First's impact and urgency matrix, she assigns the ticket a priority of 3 (like most IT service desks, tickets are assigned a priority from 1 to 4, with 1 being the highest priority).

At Fly First there are no service level penalties for priority-3 incidents and there is a KPI of a 5-day resolution.

To try to help Carmen get the counter working, Sue also searches knowledge articles to determine whether this issue has happened before and whether there's a workaround. She advises Carmen to try turning the counter off and on. Carmen has already tried that, but to no avail.

Ticket is assigned to a resolver group

Sue then assigns the ticket to the level-2 internal resolver group responsible for printing devices. According to the incident management process, Sue has completed her job perfectly. She's even managed to meet her KPI on call-handling time.

When the resolver group receives the low-priority ticket, the team is already busy with higher-priority tickets and working on business-as-usual activities; Carmen's issue sits in the queue. Meanwhile, Carmen is getting more and more frustrated. Some bags have already gone through to the baggage handling area with the wrong destinations printed on their tags! She asks her team to check every bag tag. More than one counter is now printing the incorrect destination, and the line of frustrated passengers is growing.

When a member of the IT printing team opens the ticket, they attempt to contact Carmen, but she is busy assisting her passengers. After two unsuccessful attempts, Carmen answers the call. She is overwhelmed and becomes increasingly frustrated at the questions being asked: 'Have you turned the counters off and on?' 'Is there paper in the printer?' You can imagine how she feels being asked these questions in this high-pressure situation.

The resolver group performs further triaging and determines that this isn't a printer issue. It could be an application or middleware issue, requiring the ticket to be re-assigned to another resolver group – both the application and middleware of the baggage ticketing system are outsourced.

Ticket is re-assigned

The ticket is re-assigned to the IT service desk. Amanda from the service desk opens the ticket; it is next in the queue. She is new to Fly First and doesn't understand the issue. She consults Sue, who advises her to assign the ticket to the application team. Sue also advises Amanda that she will need to send an email (the new IT service management tool at Fly First doesn't have integration between suppliers – unfortunately the new IT service management tooling project budget was cut). Both Sue's and Amanda's KPIs are now at risk – their ticket re-assignment count and resolution times are about to be breached. Meanwhile, Carmen's ticket is re-assigned back and forth between IT resolver groups for several hours.

Ticket is assigned a higher priority

Following a further call from Carmen to the IT service desk, the ticket has now been assigned a higher priority.

Issue resolved

A while later, the supplier responsible for the application fixes the issue. The issue was due to a failed software change the previous evening – the baggage check-in counters are now printing the correct destinations.

Close ticket

Adhering to Fly First's incident management process, before the ticket can be closed, a member of the IT service desk attempts to contact Carmen to verify that the counters are working correctly. Carmen has finished her shift, and the afternoon airport supervisor, Tommy, takes the call from their shared mobile phone. Following some confusion (it was Carmen who logged the ticket), Tommy confirms that the counters are working, and the ticket is closed. An automated customer survey from the IT service desk is sent to Carmen's email address, but she has gone on two weeks' leave.

In the monthly service level governance report, the supplier for the application is able to report that there have been no breaches of service levels: the availability and response service levels have been met. The system was available all the time, and the bag tags were being printed in a timely manner!

 Key message

Every person in IT followed the correct process as outlined in the Fly First incident management process. However, the outcome resulted in a poor experience for Carmen, Sue, the IT support staff, and Fly First's passengers.

Over to you

What was the customer journey?

Can you identify the business value stream Carmen was performing to support the customer journey?

Which IT service management value streams should be used to support Carmen, her team and the IT support professionals?

Using the skills we learnt in Chapter 6, map the three layers of Humanising IT for the value streams you have identified:

- Customer layer
- Business layer
- IT service management layer.

What steps can you identify that the IT service desk should have taken to ensure the ticket was assigned to the correct resolver group when Carmen first contacted the desk?

Can you identify three actions that would have improved how the issue was handled?

Who do you think is responsible for Carmen's less-than-optimum experience when dealing with IT?

Human-centred design for IT service management

Index

added value 10

Babbage, Charles 16
baggage handling 48
Berners-Lee, Tim 16
best practices 22, 23, 84
blueprinting 143–148
brainstorming 56
break/fix operating model 69–70
business outcomes 11, 13
business relationship management 117–119
business services 65
business value streams 123, 126–128, 135 see also
    value streams

call duration 36
Capability Maturity Model 36–37
cars 74
change 115–116
collaboration 56
collaborative teams 59–60
confirmation bias 96–97
confusion, cost of 6–7
convergent thinking 91–93, 95
cost of confusion 6–7
Covid-19 pandemic 72
creativity 55–56
current state maps 105–106
customer focus 68–69
customer journey maps 138–143
customers 30, 44, 65, 119

data 97
design 40
divergent thinking 91–93, 95
Double Diamond model
    define phase 79–82, 90, 104–109
    deliver phase 83, 90, 112–114
    develop phase 83, 90, 109–112
    discovery phase 79, 90, 100–103
    and human-centred design 85
    and IT value chain 78–83
DVF checklist 60–61
DVF model 57–59

efficiency 33
empathy 40–49, 127, 146–147
    case study 48
    definition 41
    drawbacks 46
    and observation 45–48
    user guide 43–44
empathy maps 102–103
evidence 99

feedback 97
five Ps of human-centred design 60, 76–77, 85
Fly First Airlines
    bag tag issue 153–155
    business outcomes 11, 122–123
    business value streams 128
    personas 51–52

proto-personas 54
    reframing 80
Ford, Henry 45
Fordism 20–22
four Ps of IT service management (ITSM) 75–76, 85
future state maps 107

happy paths 127, 135
healthcare 108–109, 128
HiPPO syndrome 106
home working 72
hospitals 13–15
how-might-we technique 81, 82
human experience agreements 70–71
human needs 39
human-centred design 27–28, 30, 39–61
    and change 115–116
    definition 2
    and environment 77
    evidence-based 99
    five Ps 60, 76–77, 85
    integration with IT service management (ITSM) 63–87
    origins of 56–57
    purpose of 77

ideation 110–111
IDEO 43
incident management 5, 23–26, 82
incidents 28–29
inefficiency 33
insights 97–98
intensive care 108–109
internet 16
IT culture 3
IT departments
    business view of 4–5
    extension of 10
    history of 8
IT service desk analysts 34–35, 138
IT service desks 33–36, 138
IT service management (ITSM)
    break/fix operating model 69–70
    and business outcomes 13
    business relationship management 117–119
    definition 2, 64, 66, 68
    disconnect from business 8
    evolution of 23
    experience of 10
    four Ps 75–76, 85
    humanising 1–2, 27–28, 149–150
    improvement 15
    integration with human-centred design 63–87
    layer 147–150
    measurement of 31–33
    one-size-fits-all approach 19, 22
    perception of 9
    processes 123–125
    reliance on 15
    strategic role of 9
    value stream mapping 121, 125–126
IT service management value streams 128, 135–136
    see also value streams

IT services 64
IT support analysts 34–35
IT value chains 78–79, 84, 85, 121–122
iteration 113–114
ITSM *see* IT service management

Kennedy, John F. 12
key user groups 54–55

lines of interaction 144

measurement of ITSM 31–33
mission statements 11
Model T Ford 19–22
moon landings 12

NASA 12
needs 39

observation and empathy 45–48
one-size-fits-all approach to incident management 23–26
one-size-fits-all approach to ITSM 19, *22*
on-time performance (OTP) 11

participatory design 56–57
peanut butter sandwiches 128–134, 146
perception 9
personas 49–54
Plato 57
problem definition 105, 107
problems 28
processes 123–125
proto-personas 52–54

qualitative research 95, 96
quantitative research 95–96

reframing 79–81
research 95–96
restaurants 120

service 1
service blueprints 143–148
service level agreements 70–71
service value chains 78–79, 84, 85, 121–122
storytelling 141
swivel chairing 34
synthesis 104

Taylorism 20
technology 1, 16–17
theatre 136–138
toothbrushes 42
transformation 115–116
triple bottom line 77

unhappy paths 127, 135
user acceptance testing 113
users 24–26, 30, 44, 59–60, 65, 119

value co-creation 94
value stream mapping 121, 125–126, 127, 148
value streams
    definition 121
    design 117–151
    examples of 122–123
    and human experience 135

humanising 135–136, 149–150
peanut butter sandwiches 128
theatre 136–138
visualization 141

Human-centred design for IT service management

Human-centred design for IT service management